"For readers who really don't know the Bible well (and hate to admit it), John Goldingay's well-written, concise outline is utterly accessible and complete. It's just the tool we need. As a skilled teacher of the Old Testament, he knows how often everyone can be overwhelmed by the details. This reader's guide provides the brief summaries we need to grasp the larger story arc and its essential teachings. I can imagine this book being widely used in churches or as a review for students who need to complete what they're missing."

Gary M. Burge, professor of New Testament, Calvin Theological Seminary

"John Goldingay pours the wisdom of years of scholarship and teaching into this primer on the Bible. He invites us into the world of this ancient text to hear how it tells the story of God and God's people. *A Reader's Guide to the Bible* provides a straightforward and succinct point of entry for anyone desiring better acquaintance with the Bible. I cannot recommend this little volume highly enough."

Jeannine K. Brown, professor of New Testament, Bethel Seminary

"The Bible can be overwhelming for the first-time reader. There's so much to take in, so much to fill in ('Where in the story does this prophet fit in?'), and so much to coordinate (like two versions of the story of Israel's monarchy and four versions of the story of Jesus). Having devoted his career equally to the scholarly study of Scripture among academics and to the communication of its message to 'normal' people, Goldingay now offers a primer for those furthest from being at home in the pages of the Bible. This book provides a winsome overview of the story of the whole and how all the parts fit together. It's an ideal tool for the person standing at the threshold of his or her first time reading through the Bible itself."

David A. deSilva, author of *Day of Atonement*

"Whether you're setting out to explore the world of the Bible for the first time or are a seasoned traveler, this brief guide is a trustworthy companion. Old Testament scholar John Goldingay knows the ins and outs of Scripture but limits himself to information and themes that will enhance your own exploration."

Lindsay Olesberg, Scripture engagement director, InterVarsity Christian Fellowship, author of *The Bible Study Handbook*

"John Goldingay shows us how the Israelites found themselves in God's story and invites us to find ourselves in it too. He lays out a framework for reading the Bible as well as an interpretive lens through which to understand each book in its context. In doing so, Goldingay invites us to dive deeper into the individual books of the Bible, but also into the rich life behind the texts. We are enchanted by the story of God at work among his people, seeing how our Lord has been weaving a redemptive narrative from the start. Even those who have been reading Scripture for decades will learn fresh ways of approaching the text."

Annie Neufeld, pastor, Lake Avenue Church, Pasadena, California

"*A Reader's Guide to the Bible* is a thorough and user-friendly outline of the story of God. A brilliant academic exposition that transcends the world of academia. This book can be read by both the seminarian and the one completely new to their faith. A must-have for anyone wanting a more thorough understanding of what the Bible is."

Albert Tate, senior pastor, Fellowship Monrovia

"Whether you're new to the Bible or have been reading it for years, John Goldingay's *A Reader's Guide to the Bible* will prove a helpful companion as you turn the pages of the world's bestselling book. Concise, accessible, and insightful, Goldingay provides the reader with an introduction to the stories, cultures, and history from which the Bible arises, serving to deepen our understanding of the story of God unfolding in its pages."

Sean Gladding, author of *Ten* and *The Story of God, the Story of Us*

A READER'S GUIDE TO THE BIBLE

JOHN GOLDINGAY

IVP Academic

An imprint of InterVarsity Press
Downers Grove, Illinois

InterVarsity Press
P.O. Box 1400, Downers Grove, IL 60515-1426
ivpress.com
email@ivpress.com

InterVarsity Press® is the book-publishing division of InterVarsity Christian Fellowship/USA®, a movement of students and faculty active on campus at hundreds of universities, colleges, and schools of nursing in the United States of America, and a member movement of the International Fellowship of Evangelical Students. For information about local and regional activities, visit intervarsity.org.

All Scripture quotations, unless otherwise indicated, are the author's translation.

Cover design: Cindy Kiple
Interior design: Jeanna Wiggins
Images: © Educester/iStockphoto

ISBN 978-0-8308-5174-4 (print)
ISBN 978-0-8308-9286-0 (digital)

Printed in the United States of America ∞

InterVarsity Press is committed to ecological stewardship and to the conservation of natural resources in all our operations. This book was printed using sustainably sourced paper.

Library of Congress Cataloging-in-Publication Data
A catalog record for this book is available from the Library of Congress.

P	25	24	23	22	21	20	19	18	17	16	15	14	13	12	11	10	9	8	7	6	5	4	3	2	1
Y	36	35	34	33	32	31	30	29	28	27	26	25	24	23	22	21	20	19	18	17					

CONTENTS

PART I

GOD'S STORY AND GOD'S WORD IN GOD'S WORLD

T HE BIBLE IS MORE A SHELF OF BOOKS than merely one volume: it's a collection of sixty-six compositions, of varied size, covering a thousand years and more. They were written in the Middle East and around the Mediterranean, and they use three languages, Hebrew (for most of them); Aramaic (for some chapters of Ezra and Daniel), a sister language of Hebrew, which probably Jesus spoke; and Greek (for the latest of the books).

The Hebrew and Aramaic books are called by Jews "The Torah, the Prophets, and the Writings"; to a Jew these are "the Scriptures." Christians refer to them as the "Old Testament" because they add to them the "New Testament," the books written in Greek (though also written by Jews). Christianity places most emphasis on these later writings and often uses them to provide the key to understanding the earlier writings.

In this book, after three introductory chapters, we are going to look at the Bible mainly as "God's story" and as "God's word." We begin with the story that starts with creation and takes the people of God down to the end of their independent political existence in 587 BC (chaps. 4–5). Then we look at a retold version of the story that centers its interest in Israel's worship (chap. 6) and at some shorter stories (chap. 7) before coming to what Christians see as the climax of the story in Jesus of Nazareth (chap. 8).

Other parts of the Bible do not have the narrative form of the story: rather, they explicitly teach or preach. Thus we look in successive chapters at law, prophecy, advice, letter writing, and visions (chaps. 9–13). Then, after two chapters considering Israel's response in the form of its worship and its intellectual wrestling (chaps. 14–15) we ask the question, How can the Bible speak today (chap. 16)?

The books collected into the Old and New Testaments are not the only old Jewish and Christian writings we have; the ones included here are those included in Protestant Bibles. The Bible as read by Catholic and Orthodox Christians includes some other Jewish writings, the "Apocrypha" or "Deuterocanonical Books." These belong to the period from the time of the latest Old Testament books up to that of the New Testament. They provide more examples of the kind of writings we look at here: further accounts of the story of the nation and further short stories (Tobit, Judith, Maccabees, 1 Esdras), as well as additions to the earlier stories and further visions (2 Esdras), two more wisdom books (Wisdom and Ecclesiasticus), and a further psalm (the Prayer of Manasseh). Baruch is more difficult to classify: it has affinities with story, prophecy, psalmody, and wisdom.

The Bible is God's book. God was involved in its coming into being, and it tells us the truth about God and about us. It's also a human book. When God first created the world, he did it without human help. He said "let there be light"—and there was light. He could have created the Bible the same way, no doubt. It could have dropped straight from heaven. In fact it was written by human beings—people such as Isaiah and Matthew. God worked through them and spoke to them, but the books are their work too. This doesn't mean it's spoiled by being a human book. It does mean that if we want to understand it, we'll need sympathy both for the God behind it and for the human beings behind it. You don't have to believe in God to understand the Bible. You do have to be sympathetic to the way it talks about God and about the world as his world. You have to have an open mind. You have to try to look at life the way the Bible does, if you are to understand it. You also have to have sympathy for the people behind it. You are not a farmer in Hebron in 800 BC, or a scribe in Babylon in 400 BC, or a slave in Rome in AD 50. But you have to imagine how life was for them, if you are to understand the books they wrote or the books they read.

THE EVENTS
OF THE BIBLE

ORIGINS (?2000–1200 BEFORE CHRIST)

The first date we can be reasonably sure of in the Bible is when some Israelites escaped from labor camps in Egypt under the leadership of Moses; the time is about 1260. But the Israelites regarded the beginning of their story as the journey of Abraham and Sarah from Mesopotamia to Canaan. Mesopotamia means "between the rivers," and it denotes the country between the Rivers Tigris and Euphrates, seven hundred miles east of Palestine. It overlaps with the modern states of Iraq and Iran stretching down to the Persian Gulf.

One of the oldest and most splendid cities of Mesopotamia was Ur of the Chaldees. *Chaldea* is another word for Babylonia. Genesis tells us that, for reasons it doesn't say, a man named Terah, with his wives and family, left Ur and traveled northwest to the town of Haran. After Terah's death, part of the family, headed by his son Abraham, left Haran and migrated in a southwesterly direction toward the land of the Canaanites.

Racially, Abraham's clan and the inhabitants of Canaan were related; their languages, too, were similar. They would be quite able to communicate with one another. However, their cultures and ways of life were different. The Canaanites were a settled, agricultural people. They worshiped a variety of gods under the presidency of one named El, who had sanctuaries throughout the country. Abraham's clan were shepherds, not farmers, and they were thus less used to staying in one place: they might wander as they wished, and indeed they were obliged to wander to some extent, ever in search of pasturage for their flocks. Their God guided the leader of the clan and was thus often called by the name of the leader, by names such as "the God of Abraham." This God accompanied them on their travels.

So Abraham and Sarah, Isaac and Rebecca, Jacob and his twelve sons moved to Canaan. They might have carried on living as shepherds there had it not been for a desperate famine that took Abraham's great-grandchildren to Egypt. There, in fact, they settled and lived happily, until there was a change of government and a king (or pharaoh) came to the throne who was not so sympathetic to these aliens in his country.

So by about 1300 the descendants of Jacob—who had been given the new name "Israel"—were no better than state serfs of the Egyptians. At this time there were various Semite groups in Egypt, many of whom were put to work on building projects in the Delta area. However, one group fled from there, led by Moses. They raced east toward the Sinai Peninsula, and after a miraculous escape near the site of the present Suez Canal, found refuge in the desert. It was an area Moses knew well, and he led them to the mountain where the God of Abraham had once appeared to him. There a pact was made between God and this people, Israel.

The pact is referred to in the Bible as a "covenant." The word denotes a solemn commitment. In this case, it is a two-sided agreement by which two parties promise to be faithful to each other. God had reached out to the Israelites, and now they committed themselves to God. The Ten Commandments and God's other instructions are the standard that Israel agreed to accept as their part in keeping the covenant (though we do not know how many of these instructions go back to Sinai).

On leaving Sinai to move on to their destination in Canaan, these Israelites lived as nomads for a generation, mostly in the northern part of the Sinai Peninsula. Eventually they traveled up the east side of the Jordan rift, through the countries of Edom and Moab, and crossed the River Jordan near Jericho. They won spectacular victories under Joshua in the heart of the country, and these victories impressed themselves on later generations as the key to the Israelites' occupation of the country as a whole. But before Joshua's victories, the Israelites had conquered the country east of the Jordan separately, and the territory that became Judah was apparently attacked from the south by Caleb. Even in the center and north, some of the peoples of Canaan accepted the invaders, without resistance, perhaps recognizing them as their own kin and acknowledging the invaders' God as their own too. One way and another, Israel could claim possession of the hill country west of the Jordan and of a fair slice of territory on the other side.

The following parts of the Bible refer to these events:

◆ Israel's ancestors	Genesis (Job is also set in this period)
◆ The exodus	Exodus 1–18
◆ The covenant at Sinai	Exodus 19–40; Leviticus; Numbers 1–10

- The time of wandering   Numbers 11–36;
  Deuteronomy
- The conquest under Joshua   Joshua

Chaos and Kingship (1200–931 Before Christ)

The story of Israel's getting into Canaan ought to lead into "and lived happily ever after." In fact, it's only the beginning of Israel's troubles. Many Canaanite clans had not been defeated by the Israelites. Even the later capital, Jerusalem, was still controlled by an indigenous people called the Jebusites. Furthermore, at about the same time as the Israelites were making inroads on Canaanite territory from the east, the Philistines (who came originally from across the Mediterranean) were doing the same from the west. While the Canaanites might be doomed by this pincer movement, it was not clear that Israel would be the eventual victor.

In another way, the Canaanites themselves formed an even more serious threat to Israel. Their religion had a beguiling attraction for the Israelites. The name of the Israelites' God was Yhwh, probably pronounced "Yahweh" (it used to be misspelled as "Jehovah") and represented in most English Bibles by the phrase "the Lord." This God had proved powerful in meeting the people's needs in rescuing them from oppression and aiding them in battle. But could this God make crops grow? There might be doubt about that. On the other hand, making crops grow was the specialty of the Canaanite god Baal (El's son)—so his worshipers claimed. And often Israelites fell to the temptation to join in his worship. Moral chaos also characterized these early years in Palestine: "all the people did what was right in their own eyes" (Judg 21:25).

Renowned leaders such as Deborah, Gideon, Samson, and Samuel belong to this period. They are often referred to as the "judges," though the title is misleading because they were primarily figures through whom God rescued the people from apostasy and oppression. But the Israelites never won final security. With the Philistine threat increasing and Samuel now old, the Israelites eventually insisted on having the organized leadership required by the challenge of the situation. They insisted on having kings, like everyone else.

The first king was Saul, who won notable victories, though without being able to deal with the Philistine threat. Nor did he deal with the problem of religious anarchy: indeed he perhaps contributed to the problem by the shortcomings in his own commitment to Yahweh. He died in battle with the Philistines.

Even in Saul's lifetime a younger man named David, a southerner (unlike Saul), had been cutting a more impressive figure. He was soon made king over the southern clans and eventually, when the family and followers of Saul were eliminated, over the northern clans too.

David was a key figure in Israel's history. He disposed of the Philistine threat and created an empire that for his lifetime dominated the area on both sides of the Jordan. He captured Jerusalem and there installed the covenant chest or ark, a symbol of God's presence that went back to the time at Sinai. His innovations mark a significant stage in the development of Israel's worship, and the musical tradition of the temple (especially psalmody) was later traced back to him, though the building of the temple was not to be put into effect in his lifetime.

In the area of personal relations, however, he was weak, and in particular he never properly handled the key question of who was to be his successor. Eventually Solomon emerged; the actual building of the temple was his achievement. He is also credited with encouraging the teaching of "wisdom" in Israel, particularly as this is represented in the advice on everyday life offered by Proverbs; and it has been hypothesized that the cultural development belonging to his reign included the writing of the first connected history of Israel. However, he was unable to do more than hang on precariously to the Davidic empire, and in his reign the weaknesses that were to destroy the state became clear.

The following parts of the Bible refer to this period:

* The judges and Saul   Judges; 1 Samuel
* David   2 Samuel; 1 Chronicles; Psalms
* Solomon   I Kings 1–11; 2 Chronicles 1–9; Proverbs

DECLINE AND FALL (931–587 BEFORE CHRIST)

Solomon was a statesman, and it was part of his undoing; he was willing to compromise over questions of faith in "the national interest." His son Rehoboam was not a statesman, and it was his undoing. While conditions in Palestine had militated against the clans really being one nation until they were united by a king, that fragile unity now disintegrated. Rehoboam lost the allegiance of virtually all the clans except his own, Judah. Thus from now on there were two independent states, Judah in the south (ruled by a descendant of David), and in the north, the main body of the clans, who inherited the title "Israel" but can also be referred to as Ephraim (which is less confusing). Jerusalem remained in Judah; it was now at the extreme northern end of its kingdom.

The story of Ephraim is short and bloody. Its first king, Jeroboam, made an astute midwife for the new state, though he is condemned for establishing sanctuaries to replace Jerusalem in his people's affections. His son Nadab was assassinated and succeeded by

Baasha. His son Elah was also assassinated and succeeded by one of his generals, Zimri, who was in turn soon overthrown in another coup and replaced by the army chief of staff, Omri. Omri was the greatest of Ephraim's kings; he was responsible for the building of its permanent capital, Samaria. His son Ahab, husband of Jezebel, was hounded by the first great prophet known to us, Elijah, on account of the religious and social horrors that increasingly characterized Ephraim. The lifetimes of Elijah and his successor, Elisha, also saw the beginning of external troubles for Ephraim in the attacks by the Syrians and other smaller nations, during the time of Ahab and his sons, Ahaziah and Jehoram (Joram). Elisha then instigated another army coup; one of the generals, Jehu, eliminated Jehoram, his mother, and the rest of Ahab's family, and reformed Ephraim's religion. Jehu's descendants, Jehoahaz, Jehoash (Joash), another Jeroboam, and Zechariah, made his line the longest to last in Ephraim, but it was finally ended when Zechariah was assassinated by Shallum, who was then shortly removed by Menahem.

Menahem's reign sees the death knell begin to ring for Ephraim. The Assyrians, who had created an empire in Mesopotamia, began to turn their mind to the west. Ephraim became their vassal. Menahem's son Pekahiah was killed by a general called Pekah, and Pekah was killed by Hoshea. During their century, the first prophets to have books named after them, Amos and Hosea, began to warn Ephraim that continuing religious apostasy and social unrighteousness would bring judgment. But the message was not heeded, and in 722 Samaria fell to the Assyrians. The Ephraimites were deported and their land settled by peoples who had been the victims of Assyrian conquest elsewhere. The northern clans virtually ceased to exist.

During this tumultuous history of the northern kingdom, the history of Judah was internally and externally much less eventful. The line of David held the throne till the end of the state's existence, even after the assassination of individuals in that line such as Joash and his son Amaziah. Judah was weaker than Ephraim and was often under pressure from its big brother to the north. Another note that recurs in its story is the question of how far it was faithful to Yahweh, and how far the kings failed to walk in David's ways. Even in this matter it proved less susceptible than Ephraim to being led astray. Judah was more isolated (by the steepness of its mountain slopes, for instance), more cut off from the likely mainstream of history. Ephraim fell first partly because its position exposed it to greater pressure.

The rise of Assyria and the appearance of the classical prophets did also affect Judah. Isaiah declared that Assyria was a greater threat to it than Syria and Ephraim, and in the time of Hezekiah Judah almost fell to the Assyrians. Hezekiah's successor, Manasseh, is regarded as the lowest apostate who ever occupied Judah's throne, and the effects of his policies could not be eradicated even by the great reformer Josiah, who followed him. The end of the sixth century saw Assyria itself fall. Judah's next overlord was Babylon, whom it had failed to take seriously enough, and in 587, after serious warnings, the Babylonians devastated Jerusalem and introduced direct rule.

The following parts of the Bible refer to this period:

+ 1 Kings 12 through 2 Kings 25

+ 2 Chronicles 10–36

+ Amos; Hosea; Isaiah 1–39; Micah

+ Nahum; Zephaniah; Habakkuk; Jeremiah

VASSAL OF BABYLON AND PERSIA
(587–333 BEFORE CHRIST)

The exiles of Judah were more fortunate than the exiles of Ephraim had been. Babylonian policy was to remove only the leaders of troublesome nations, not to transport whole peoples, and the Judahite politicians, princes, and priests were able to lead a tolerable life in Babylon. Indeed, in some ways the bulk of the ordinary population, left behind leaderless in the devastated land of Judah, were less fortunate. The five poems in Lamentations give us some idea of their feelings. Many people left Judah voluntarily; the process of their spreading all over the world had begun. Eventually the worship of the synagogue, concentrating on prayer and the reading of the Scriptures, developed, perhaps initially in Babylon. This helped to make up for separation from the temple and played an important part in keeping the people of Israel in being when they were not in their own land.

The books of Kings were compiled at the time of the exile, and by telling the story of Ephraim's and Judah's sin they comprise an acknowledgment that the exile had to happen. But even before the catastrophe, prophets such as Jeremiah (in Jerusalem) and Ezekiel (already transported to Babylon in 597) had been promising that, although the crisis had to be undergone and a long exile experienced, there would be a return to the land. The signal that this day was imminent was the growth of the Persian Empire under Cyrus, referred to in Isaiah 45. In 539 Cyrus put an end to the Babylonian Empire and allowed the various captives there, including the people of Judah, to return home.

Apparently the Judahites were in no hurry to go back to far-off, primitive Canaan, but some did so; for those who did not, involuntary exile became the voluntary dispersion that has characterized the Jewish people ever since. Between 520 and 516 the temple in Jerusalem was rebuilt under the leadership of Joshua, the high priest, and Zerubbabel, a descendant of David, though he did not occupy the throne to which he could have been a legitimate heir. Indeed, Judah did not have its own kings again for over three centuries. The rebuilding of the temple marks the beginning of the Second Temple period, which goes down to New Testament times. The priests and, later, the scribes became the leaders of the postexilic community, which was ruled by the word of the Torah. The prophecies of Haggai and Zechariah reflect how hard life was in Joshua and Zerubbabel's time. Haggai and Zechariah were almost the last prophets whose words were preserved in their names.

The Old Testament includes no connected history of the Persian era, and we know concretely about only one subsequent part of this period, the activities of Ezra and Nehemiah, who came to Jerusalem from the dispersion in the middle of the fifth century. (Note that they were not involved in the "return from the exile" and the rebuilding of the temple, which happened long before their day.) Ezra got the Persian king to commission him to go to see that religious matters were being conducted in the proper way in Jerusalem, in accordance with a scroll of the Torah that he took from Babylon. He initiated reforms there, especially to preserve the Judahite people's distinctiveness and their commitment to Yahweh. Nehemiah's activity overlapped with Ezra's. His visit to Jerusalem was prompted by news that the physical devastation of the previous century had not yet been repaired. He was responsible for rebuilding the defenses of the city, as well as for social and religious reforms.

Predictably, the rebuilding of the walls aroused the opposition of other peoples living in the area, and tension between the Judahites and related groups is a feature of this period. In particular, an animosity developed between Judahites and Samarians.

The attitudes of the people in the postexilic period can be inferred from the writings of this time. If we do not have the names of notable prophets after Malachi, nevertheless many treasured the message of the prophets and longed for the time when Yahweh would again act in history, restore Israel and endow it with the splendor the prophets spoke of, and draw the world to acknowledge Yahweh and Israel. Other people found it hard to make sense of the old faith, and Job and Qohelet (Ecclesiastes) reflect their doubts and uncertainties. Yet others tried hard to see what God was doing and what God required. The books of Chronicles belong to this period; they retell Israel's story with a focus on the temple and its services: the worship of the people of God is regarded as very important. The final editing of the first five books of the Bible, the Pentateuch, also belongs in this time, and a delight in God's Torah and a concern to obey God in every detail of life characterize the years after the exile.

The following parts of the Bible refer to this period:

+ Lamentations
+ Ezekiel; Isaiah 40–66; Daniel
+ Haggai; Zechariah; Malachi
+ Ezra-Nehemiah

PROVINCE OF GREECE AND ROME
(333 BEFORE CHRIST–135 AFTER CHRIST)

The rule of the Persians was ended by the triumph of the Greeks under Alexander the Great. In 332 Alexander passed through

Palestine on his way to Egypt; Judah probably escaped actual invasion, again because of its out-of-the-way position.

Alexander's empire lasted only a decade. In 323 he died, and his generals fought over his empire. The area north of Palestine was then ruled by Seleucus and his descendants; Egypt, to the south, was controlled by the Ptolemies. Judah found itself a buffer state.

Assyria and Babylon had attempted to crush the national aspirations of conquered peoples by transporting their people, while the Persians encouraged a positive attitude to their rule by their support of people's religious idiosyncrasies (provided these were harmless). The Greeks imported a culture that influenced their empire more than the Babylonians or Persians ever did. Jews in Alexandria, Egypt, a very Hellenistic city, translated their Bible into Greek (the Septuagint) and began actually to write in Greek. Many of these Greek books were eventually included in some versions of the Christian Bible (traditionally referred to by Protestants as the Apocrypha).

But the center of Judaism remained the temple in Jerusalem, and there Judaism found itself involved in a fight for its life with Hellenism. In 198 Palestine had passed from Ptolemaic to Seleucid control, and the Seleucid king, Antiochus Epiphanes (175–163), sought to unite his empire by imposing Greek religion and culture on all his subject peoples. He banned the Jewish religion and had the Jerusalem temple turned into a shrine to Zeus; this is the original "abomination that makes desolate" referred to in Daniel 11:31. Among some of the people this provoked at first passive resistance and then armed revolt. These rebels, called the Maccabees, proved too much for the Seleucids, who never regained control of Palestine. As Daniel promised (Dan 8:25), the "little horn," Antiochus, was broken. The people of Yahweh had their independence for the first time since the rise of Assyria six centuries previously.

Greek thinking and Greek lifestyle nevertheless deeply affected the Jewish community, and this led some groups to set up alternative societies. The most radical was the Qumran community, a religious foundation established on the shores of the Dead Sea. The Pharisees sought to remain faithful to the Torah without withdrawing from Jerusalem. The Sadducees proved more adaptable to practical politics and held power in the temple.

The decline of the Seleucids in the Middle East was accompanied by the increasing power of the Romans. Eventually the Romans sent Pompey the Great to secure the eastern boundary of their empire, and in 63 he arrived in Jerusalem, ended the rule of the descendants of the Maccabees, and made Judaea part of the Roman province of Syria.

The Romans established a puppet monarchy in Palestine, the house of Herod, who as an Idumean accepted the Jewish faith. Herod "the Great" enlarged and rebuilt the temple and undertook other building projects in Jerusalem and elsewhere—including the creation of the new seaport of Caesarea (named after the emperor).

After Herod the Great's death in 4 BC, there was rebellion against Rome. None of his family were as capable as he, and eventually his kingdom was divided, with Herodian "tetrarchs" in charge in the north, and Judaea under the direct rule of Roman governors. Many Jews were hopeful that their God might intervene, but not many of them accepted the claims of any of the "messiahs" of the time. The most important of these messianic figures, Jesus of Nazareth, was executed during the Roman governorship of Pontius Pilate. Subsequently his followers continued to propagate a belief that nevertheless he was the Messiah, and both Jewish and Roman authorities found the followers of Jesus difficult to handle.

For the most part the Roman Empire was a support rather than a hindrance to the Jewish faith, and there were Jewish communities—some of whose members were of Jewish birth, some converts—all around the Mediterranean. The stability of the Roman Empire and the spread of these Jewish communities made it easier for the followers of Jesus to spread the belief that he was the Messiah through the eastern Mediterranean and beyond—though most of the believers were Gentiles. The key figure in this achievement was a Jew from Tarsus, Saul or Paul. The Christian correspondence that has survived in the New Testament, as well as the book of Acts, indicates that these Christian communities were spread through Turkey, Greece, and as far as Rome itself.

In Palestine, however, relations between Jews and Romans deteriorated. The Jews rebelled in AD 66, and Jerusalem and its temple were destroyed in AD 70. The next century saw a further rebellion, quelled in AD 135, when Jerusalem was made a Roman city from which the Jews were banned.

The following parts of the Bible refer to this period:

* Daniel
* The New Testament
* The Old Testament Apocrypha also belongs here.

Table 2.1. An outline of Old Testament history

?	Events in Genesis	
1200	1260 The exodus (Moses) 1220 The entry into the land (Joshua)	
1100	1125 The judges (e.g., Deborah)	*Israel in conflict with, e.g., Philistines*
1000	1050 Saul 1010 David	
900	970 Solomon 930 Division into two kingdoms, northern Israel (Ephraim) and Judah	*Israel Independent*
800	850 Elijah and Elisha	
700	Amos, Hosea, Micah, Isaiah ben Amoz 722 Ephraim falls to Assyria	*Assyria in control*
600	626 God summons Jeremiah 622 Josiah's reform	*Babylon in control*
	593 God summons Ezekiel 587 Jerusalem falls to Babylon 540s Isaiah 40–55 539 Babylon falls to Persia; Judahites free to return, rebuild temple	*Persia in control*
	Haggai, Zechariah, Isaiah 56-66 (Ezra 1–6, Dan 1–6)	
	Persian kings: 539 Cyrus 530 Cambyses	
500	522 Darius I	
	486 Xerxes I (Ahasuerus in Ezra 4 and Esther) 465 Artaxerxes 458 Ezra 445 Nehemiah	
400	*(The OT is coming into the form we have it c. 587–164: a resource for the Second Temple community in keeping faith and hope in tough times.)*	
300	333 Persia falls to Greece (Alexander); then the empire splits	*Greece in control*
200		
100	198 Jerusalem moves from Egyptian to Syrian control 167 Antiochus Epiphanes introduces pagan worship to temple (Daniel's visions)	*Jerusalem Independent*
	63 Pompey visits Jerusalem	*Rome in control*

Table 2.2. More detail on the history of Ephraim and Judah

Date and Foreign power	Ephraim	Prophets	Judah
1050	Saul	Samuel	Saul
1010	David	Gad, Nathan	David
970	Solomon	Ahijah	Solomon
Egypt (Shishak)	Jeroboam (22)	Unnamed men of God	Rehoboam (17)
			Abijam/Abijah (3)
	Nadab (2)		Asa (41)
Syria	Baasha (12)		
	Elah (2)		
	Zimri (one week)		
	Omri (12)		
	Ahab (22)	Elijah	Jehoshaphat (25)
	Ahaziah (2)		
	Jehoram/Joram (12)	Elisha	Jehoram/Joram (8)
			Ahaziah (1)
			Athaliah (7)
	Jehu (28)	?Joel	Jehoash/Joash (16)
	Jehoahaz (17)	Jonah	
Assyria	Jehoash/Joash	Hosea	
	Jeroboam II (41)	Amos	Amaziah (29)
	Zechariah (6m)		Uzziah/Azariah (52)
	Shallum (1m)		
	Menahem (10)		
	Pekahiah (2)		
	Pekah (20)	Jotham (16)	
	Hoshea (9)	Isaiah	Ahaz (16)
722		Micah	Hezekiah (29)
			Manasseh (55)
			Amon (2)
		Zephaniah	Josiah (31)
		Nahum	Jehoahaz/Shallum (3m)
		Jeremiah	Jehoiakim/Eliakim (11)
Babylon		Habakkuk	Jehoiachin/Coniah/
		Obadiah	Shallum (3m)
587		Ezekiel (in Babylon)	Zedekiah/Mattaniah (11)
		Isaiah 40–55 (in Babylon)	
Persia		Haggai	
539		Zechariah	
		Isaiah 56–66	
		Malachi	
		?Joel	
		?Book of Jonah	
		?Zechariah 9-14	
Greece 336			

Note: The numbers are the total lengths of reigns in years—they are all approximate and they include the period when the king co-reigned with his father or son.

2

THE LAND
OF THE BIBLE

T HREE VERY DIFFERENT AREAS form the scene of the
Bible story:

1. Mesopotamia

2. the countries that border on the Mediterranean

3. the territory between those two areas

The story begins in the powerful empires of Mesopotamia
and Africa. The flat plains of Mesopotamia are the background
of the account of the Garden of Eden, the flood, the tower of
Babel, and the origins of Abraham. It was to Babylon (modern
Iraq) that many leading Judahites were exiled in 597 and 587
BC. From then on, Babylon was an important center of Judaism.
Babylon is also a symbol of oppression. So is Egypt: in fact, the
chief importance of the land of the Nile is as the land of affliction from which the Israelites were rescued in the time of
Moses. It, too, was a place of exile from 587 and a center of
subsequent Judaism.

Egypt belongs also to the very different area where the Bible
story ends, the Mediterranean countries, when the message of

Christianity is passed on to North Africa, Turkey, Greece, Italy, and Spain. The feature of this area that distinguishes it from the east is that it centers on the sea. It was largely by sea, across the Mediterranean, that the Christian message spread. These countries belonged to the empire of the Romans, the most important political feature of the period. Rome, like Babylon and Egypt, is a symbol of oppression in the New Testament.

The Bible story focuses, however, on a third area, "the holy land," which lies between the empires of Mesopotamia, the Nile, and the Mediterranean. This area has never been the center of a major empire itself, even in the time of David and Solomon, but it has always been a cockpit of history, a buffer zone between major empires. Perhaps its position at the junction of the continents of Asia, Europe, and Africa contributes to its being a meeting point of peoples and their history.

The boundaries of this land often changed, like the boundaries of modern states. The name changed too. When the Israelites refer to its history before they arrived, they call it Canaan; later it was named Palestine (after the Philistines). Since Israel is the name of a particular state today, and Palestine may become the name of another one, in this section we will use the old name Canaan as the name of the land in which Israel lived.

Canaan is a small country. The area spoken of in the Bible includes parts of what is now Lebanon (the region of Tyre and Sidon), of Syria (the Golan) and of Jordan (Gilead, east of the Jordan), and the whole of the West Bank, which includes many of the most important towns of the Bible (Shechem, Samaria, Bethlehem, and Hebron), as well as the state of Israel. Nevertheless, from Dan to Beersheba (Israel's equivalent of from Maine to Florida) is only 150 miles. East to west, the land

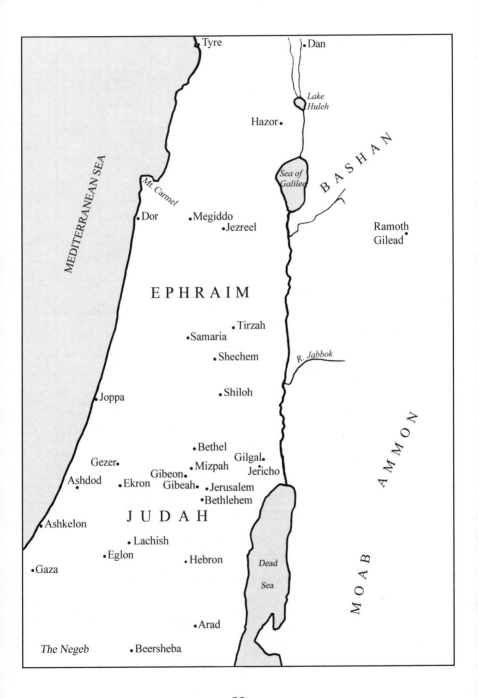

Tyre

Dan

Lake
Huleh

Hazor

Sea of
Galilee

BASHAN

Mt. Carmel

MEDITERRANEAN SEA

Dor

Megiddo

Jezreel

Ramoth
Gilead

EPHRAIM

Tirzah

Samaria

Shechem

R. Jabbok

Joppa

Shiloh

AMMON

Bethel

Gezer

Mizpah

Gilgal

Gibeon

Jericho

Ashdod

Ekron

Gibeah

Jerusalem

Bethlehem

Ashkelon

JUDAH

Lachish

Eglon

Hebron

Dead

Gaza

Sea

MOAB

Arad

The Negeb

Beersheba

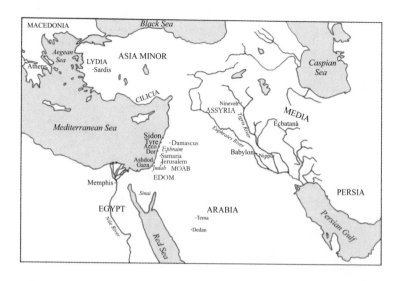

measures fifty to eighty miles. Jerusalem is only forty miles or so from either Tel Aviv or Amman.

Within this small country there is extraordinary variation. There are fertile plains on the coast and in Jezreel, but steep mountains inland, like the Atlantic coastal plain and the Appalachian Mountains. Between the mountains of Canaan and Lebanon, and those of Jordan and Syria, is the valley of the River Jordan, which in the north is shallow and rich, to the south steep and dry (except for oases such as Jericho). There is a mountain range that rises to three thousand feet and a valley that contains the lowest-lying sea on earth, and there can be at the same time snow on the former and, a few miles away, sunbaked desert around the latter. There are dry riverbeds that in winter briefly become raging torrents, and scorched hills that in spring become carpeted with flowers.

Canaan may be divided into four vertical stripes—the plains, the mountains west of the Jordan, the Jordan Valley, and the mountains east of the Jordan. Each becomes higher the farther you travel north, drier and less cultivable the farther you travel south.

THE PLAINS

For practical purposes, the most important parts of this land are the plains, which form a strip along the coast and then from the Bay of Haifa drive a wedge inland (the plain of Jezreel). Most of the main roads and railways have generally run along these plains. Much of the most fertile land is here, and fruit, cotton, and other crops are grown (though some of the land was marshy until the last century or so). But in the south, where the coastal plain is broadest and curves around the south of the mountains, it becomes desert—the Negev. Beersheba, a center as important in the time of Abraham as today, dominates this steppe area.

Many of the states that have controlled Canaan were centered on the plains. In pre- and early Israelite times the great cities of the Canaanites and the Philistines were here, such as Beth-Shean, Megiddo, Gezer, Ashkelon, and Gaza. The Romans built Caesarea on the coast by the plain, and modern times have seen substantial urban growth on the coast, especially around Tel Aviv and Haifa. It has always been the more developed nation that controlled the plain: the less advanced had to make do with the mountains.

The plain of Jezreel is the great battleground of the Bible, the scene of the victories of Deborah and Barak over the Canaanites (Judg 4) and Gideon over the Midianites (Judg 7), the scene of the deaths of Saul at the hand of the Philistines (1 Sam 31) and Josiah at the hand of the Egyptians (2 Kings 23), and the scene of the last battle to come at Armageddon (mountain of Megiddo).

In the southern half of the land the plain is separated from the mountains by hills like those in upstate New York—the "hill country" or "lowlands" in the Old Testament. This formed a natural first line of defense for Judah, especially against the Philistines, and it was the scene of exploits on the part of Joshua, Samson, and David.

ACROSS THE JORDAN

The eastern boundary of the holy land is the mountain chain that rises east of the Jordan and eventually becomes the Arabian Desert. In the far north is Mount Hermon, whose peak dwarfs all the mountains of the holy land itself into mere hillocks. To its south, and to the east and southeast of Lake Galilee, are the regions of Bashan and Gilead, once evidently a prosperous area (its cattle were renowned), but notorious more recently as a theater of war (Bashan is the Golan Heights). In New Testament times the area of Gilead was predominantly Greek and was called by the Greek name Decapolis, "Ten Cities"; Jesus journeyed there.

Across the Golan Heights runs a road from Damascus and the north and east to Lake Galilee and the south. This road marks the route of Israel's ancestors (the fords of the Jordan are named after Jacob's daughters), of Judahites going into exile and returning, and of the journey of Saul to Damascus. It was on the way down from the Golan Heights that Saul was confronted by Jesus (Acts 9).

Gilead and the plateau to the south (Ammon, then Moab, then Edom or Idumaea) belong today to the state of Jordan. Its peoples were defeated by the Israelites under Moses on the way to Canaan after the exodus (Num 20) and again at the time of Israel's greatest power by David (2 Sam 10). But they often formed a thorn in Israel's flesh.

WEST OF THE JORDAN

The center of attention in the Bible lies not in these two outer stripes, however, but primarily in the mountains west of the Jordan, in Galilee, Samaria, and Judah. Galilee in the north is mentioned rarely in the Old Testament but features in the New Testament as the home of Jesus and the scene of much of his ministry. The mountains here rise steeply from the Mediterranean on the west and from Lake Galilee in the east—though there is no shortage of feasible east-west routes across these mountains. The lake takes its name from the area, rather than the other way around, and in the Bible (and today) "Galilee" refers more often to the whole area than to the lake to the east (which is called Kinneret in the Old Testament and today). The best-known town in Galilee today is Nazareth, but in New Testament times this was an insignificant hamlet. Safed, too, the most important Jewish town in modern Galilee, has become important only in relatively recent times.

Galilee is a fertile area. A proverb says that it is easier to raise a legion of olives in Galilee than to bring up a child in Israel proper. Wheat and grapes abound also. Farther north, the hills of Galilee become the mountains of Lebanon, with their cedar forests that provided the timber for Solomon's temple.

Samaria, the center of the land, includes the towns of Shechem, Shiloh, Bethel, and modern Ramallah, as well as Omri's city of Samaria, which gave the area its name. All these cities lay on or near the ridge of the mountains that form a single range, the spine of the country as a whole, falling away to the east and west. They slope fairly gently, however, and there are several reasonably easy access routes from the plain into the mountains—especially to Shechem (modern Nablus, at the center of the northern part of the West Bank), which also has an easy route east to the Jordan and thus marks an important crossroads. Shechem was Abraham's first stopping point (Gen 12), the site of Jacob's well and of the meeting of Jesus and the Samaritan woman (Jn 4), and the site of the reading of the covenant law and of the remaking of the covenant in the time of Joshua (Josh 24).

To the north, the mountains include a spur running northwest until it tumbles into the Mediterranean at Haifa and causes the only hiccup on the straight line of coast from Lebanon to Egypt. This northwestern spur is Mount Carmel, the scene of Elijah's contest with the Baal prophets (1 Kings 18). Most north-south traffic along the plains crosses the mountains just southeast of Mount Carmel at the strategic pass guarded on the Jezreel side by Megiddo.

Samaria and Galilee belonged to the northern clans of Israel, dominated by Ephraim. These clans went independent of the south after the death of Solomon. In 722 they were conquered by the Assyrians, and many of their population were replaced by foreigners. Thus "Samaritan" came to mean religiously and racially impure; the Samaritans were halfway to being Gentiles. Similarly Galilee became known as Galilee of the Gentiles (Is 9:1). It was the far north, provincial and outcast.

Judah and Samaria correspond broadly to the West Bank, the area of Canaan west of the River Jordan that became part of the state of Jordan in 1947 and was occupied by the state of Israel in 1967. The ridge of mountains continues southwards without any very perceptible break as Samaria ceases and Judah/Judaea begins. The line of familiar locations continues—Jerusalem, Bethlehem, Hebron—and these towns, too, are places on the journeys of Abraham and his successors up and down Canaan, and on the journey taken by Joseph, Mary, and Jesus between Nazareth, Jerusalem, Bethlehem, and the south (when the family sought refuge in Egypt).

If anything distinguishes Judaea from Samaria, it is that Judaea is more isolated. The slopes to the east and west are steeper, and there are no significant cross routes south of Jerusalem; indeed, on the east there is nothing to go to, only the Dead Sea. So the eastern part of Judah is quite inhospitable, but the ridge itself and the western slopes of the mountains are well-watered. They still produce an abundance of grapes, and the giant bunch found here by Moses' spies, Joshua and Caleb (Num 13), is the symbol of the Israeli Government Tourist Office.

THE JORDAN

The last stripe of country we need to describe is the most extraordinary. The Jordan "rift" is an extensive fault in the earth's surface, a crack that extends to one thousand feet below sea level at the Dead Sea. Its beginning lies far north of Canaan, but it becomes important to us at the point where the headwaters of the Jordan emerge from the foothills of Hermon. At the point where the modern states of Israel, Lebanon, and Syria meet, full-grown streams gush from the mountain. The river is one of the very few that flow all year round, fed as it is by the snows that are still seeping through the mountain in high summer.

Near one of these streams is the Israelite town of Dan, like Bethel a religious center of Ephraim. Near another is the famous Roman town of Caesarea Philippi, the scene of Jesus' recognition as Messiah by Peter (Mt 16). Probably the mountains here were also the scene of Jesus' transfiguration before the disciples, which the Gospels describe just after the Caesarea Philippi incident.

The broad Jordan Valley rolls down, between the mountains of Galilee and the Golan, to Lake Galilee, passing the ancient Canaanite city of Hazor, from which Jabin dominated the Galilee area until the Israelites arrived (Josh 11). On the busy northern shore of the lake there were flourishing Jewish cities in the time of Jesus—Chorazim, Capernaum, Bethsaida. But they were destroyed (as he said they would be) soon after his time. As you travel down the western side of the lake you pass the scenes of Jesus' ministry and eventually the Greek city of Tiberias.

The lake itself is harp-shaped, fifteen miles long and nine miles wide. It is below sea level, and the climate is humid, though the New Testament makes no reference to the climate of this area that is so important to its story. (The Old Testament does refer sometimes to climate: for instance in its references to the sun, with its dangers, and to flash floods, which can bring an unexpected victory.) Perhaps in the humid summer months people relaxed and avoided long journeys.

South of the lake the waters become the river again and meander south through a narrower valley. Near the water there is the thick growth referred to as "jungle" in Jeremiah 12. But as the level of the land falls steadily, the surroundings become drier. The area illustrates the statement that a tree with its roots down near a river can remain fruitful, but away from this source of water it withers (Ps 1); there is no rain left in the Mediterranean winds by the time they reach the Jordan side of the mountain ridge. This part of the river was the scene of John the baptizer's ministry (Mt 3), as it had been where Elisha told Naaman to wash (2 Kings 5). The Jordan flows into the Dead Sea near Jericho (scene of Joshua's first famous victory and of Jesus' meetings with Zacchaeus and Bartimaeus, and the starting point of what was then a tortuous and dangerous road up to Jerusalem). The water never leaves this sea, except upwards by evaporation. But the minerals in the water do not evaporate; they accumulate to make the lake (40 miles long) the Dead Sea: "Salt Sea" in Hebrew. There are fresh water oases in the area at Jericho and En Gedi, but for the most part it is a dead world. The valley, as it continues waterless to the south to the Gulf of Aqaba, is called the Arabah.

It's worth trying to get a feeling of the geography and climate of Canaan, because this often contributes to an understanding of the drift of the story.

THE STORY OF
GOD AND
HIS PEOPLE

I N CHAPTER ONE WE REVIEWED the Bible's history. Now we look at the Bible's story. What's the difference?

By the Bible's history I mean the actual, unadorned events that happened between 2000 BC and AD 100: the main features of a stream of happenings that was just one among many streams (the history of the Egyptians, of the Greeks, of Britain, of the United States, and so on). I tried to describe these events as factually as possible, to note the political and social developments, to set the story on the wide canvas of the international events of the period. I avoided theology (there was little mention of God) and morals (I didn't suggest that anyone ought not to have acted as they did). In this way, the history of the Jewish people or of the Christian church can be written as factually as the history of the Arabs or of a political party—though in all these examples the biases of the writers and of their age will appear.

Such objective history is not what the Bible seeks to give. In this sense, it is a mistake to treat the Bible as a history book.

Having said that, I must immediately add that it is a book of history in the sense that the story it relates is one that happened. It is not like Hans Andersen; it is not a novel. Many of the events it records are also mentioned by other ancient writings. For instance, the Babylonians left their own account of the capture of Jerusalem; the Romans found cause to refer to Jesus of Nazareth. The Bible itself emphasizes that the events in its story really happened. It was because their God did things that the Israelites could know he was really God. It was because Jesus rose from the dead that his disciples challenged people to believe in him.

Nevertheless, the story in which the account of these events is given is not written as history as it is written in the West today. The writers are not interested in what was of mere "historical" significance. They are not interested in politics or culture or social developments for their own sake. They are interested in what God was doing with his people, in how people were responding to God, and in the lessons that this story has for their readers. They are concerned to communicate, to make the story interesting, to make it intelligible for the sake of later readers, and to show them how it is significant for them.

It may be natural to modern Westerners to keep asking the question "Did it really happen?" or alternatively "Did they really think it happened?" (if we know, or think we know, that it cannot have happened). Did the serpent get on its hind legs and speak? Did the walls of Jericho fall? Did the whale swallow Jonah? Often it is impossible to answer these questions, and we must be content with a different approach. The writers imply that their story is basically historical, but they invite us to respond to it as it stands as a story, to see what it means and what it has to say.

So one key way by which the Bible writers communicated God's message to their day was by telling a story. The same stories came to be retold several times, because different lessons needed to be drawn out of them. Thus there are four Gospels in the New Testament, each with a different emphasis and message. There are two accounts of the history from David to the exile, in Samuel-Kings and Chronicles, two accounts written to bring different messages to different periods (the time of the exile itself and the period after God's people had returned from exile).

There were also more than one account of the story from creation to Moses, though these were combined into one in the first four books of the Bible. The indication that this process happened is that the books often repeat themselves: for instance, we are twice told about creation itself (Gen 1–2), and twice about God's revealing his name to Moses (Ex 3; 6). These repetitions are clues to the interweaving of two versions of the story, as in Christian times people have interwoven the four Gospels into one narrative so that people can read "the whole story" of Jesus in one book.

Some of the threads that make up the first five books in the Bible can be unwoven, and we can then see how the story was applied to the people in different periods. We will note some examples of this below. But it is a delicate exercise, and it is guesswork. Since only the conflated version has been preserved, we concentrate on that.

3

BEGINNINGS

Genesis to Numbers

T HE FIRST FIVE BOOKS OF THE BIBLE are "the Torah" (to Jews) and traditionally "the five books of Moses" (to Christians). They do not claim to have been written by Moses; titles such as "the first book of Moses" in old English translations are not part of the Bible text, and they do not appear in Hebrew Bibles. But Moses does dominate these books, and he will be the ultimate origin of the information they contain about the events related by Exodus to Deuteronomy. (Moses does not appear in Genesis.)

While the Torah sees the first *five* books together, it is the book of Joshua that marks the point where God's keeping of his promises to Israel's ancestors is brought to fulfillment, and in a sense the first *six* books belong together:

- Genesis 1–11: The beginnings of the world
- Genesis 12–50: The prehistory of Israel—God's promises given
- Exodus 1–18: Israel's deliverance from Egypt (with some instructions)

- [Exodus 19–40; Leviticus; Numbers 1–10: instructions at Sinai (with some narrative)]

- Numbers 10–36: Israel's journey toward Canaan (with some instructions)

- [Deuteronomy: instructions given beyond the Jordan (with some narrative)]

- Joshua: Israel's entry into Canaan—God's promises fulfilled

Table 4.1. An outline of the story in Genesis to Kings

Introduction	Israel's origins	How Israel's story nearly got derailed	Israel's story in the land
Genesis 1–11	God's promise Genesis 12–50		
	The fulfillment (a) The exodus Exodus 1–18		
	(b) The covenant Exodus 19– Numbers 10	A generation's delay Numbers 11– Deuteronomy	
	(c) The land Joshua		Problems in the land: Judges–1 Samuel 7
			Solution: central government and worship 1 Samuel 8–1 Kings 12
			Failure of the solution: government deposed, temple destroyed 1 Kings 13–2 Kings 25

The Hebrew word *torah* is often translated "law," but its meaning is broader: "teaching" is the nearest English word. As well as law, it includes the story of how Israel came to be God's people, and how they reached the borders of the land of Canaan. The narrative of God's dealings with the whole world, and in particular with Israel's ancestors, provides the framework for the books; the rules about matters such as worship come within the framework of the story. The Torah or Teaching is a story with instructions set in the midst of it.

The first stage in the Bible story thus ends with Deuteronomy and Joshua. But these two books look forward to life in the Promised Land and begin the story of life there, which is the focus of the books that come later, Judges-Samuel-Kings (see table 4.1), so in this chapter we will look at the first *four* books, Genesis to Numbers.

THE STORY OF HUMANITY (GENESIS 1–11)

The Bible begins (Gen 1–2) by picturing God's creation of the world and of humanity. God gives Adam and Eve a garden to live and work in, but they are expelled when they ignore his instruction. Their descendants struggle to cope with life east of Eden, but the situation deteriorates until God almost destroys the world. After the flood disaster, it deteriorates again, and God makes a further new start by calling a man named Abraham, the Israelites' ancestor, to follow him.

So the Bible starts with stories about the earliest history of the world and of humanity. This is surprising. No other nation's history starts from the creation of the world, but this history of Israel does. Other ancient religions had stories about creation, but they did not go on to link the story of creation to their own history in this way. Ancient and modern people kept creation and history in separate compartments. Israel links them.

We do not know when these creation stories were written. Genesis does not tell us who wrote it. But there are at least three situations to which Genesis as a whole seems to have a particular relevance.

The first is the exodus, Moses' own time. The story of creation introduces the story of redemption. The God who redeemed Israel is identified as the creator of the world. The opening chapters of Genesis describe how the created world went wrong: they look forward to the story of redemption and describe how God didn't abandon his world. As its creator he cared enough about the world to redeem it.

The link between the creation and the exodus is made via the story of Israel's ancestors Abraham and Sarah, Isaac and Rebekah, Jacob and his family (see fig. 4.1). The significance of these stories, which tell Israel's immediate prehistory, is that they record the promises of God that the act of God in the exodus fulfilled. They show that the exodus was not a random act without forethought. God had made a commitment to be Abraham's God, to make his family a nation, to give it a land—and God is fulfilling those promises.

The second situation with which we can connect Genesis is the peak of Israel's history, which was constituted by the achievements of David and Solomon. Israel has a new position in the world—it is a sizable nation, with other peoples under its sovereignty. The creation story reminds it of the limitations of power, of the lure of the serpent (an important symbol in Canaanite religion), of God's purpose for the world, of which Israel is lord. Abraham's story reminds Israel of the promise of God, which has now received a fuller fulfillment, of the links between Israel's ancestors and the city of Jerusalem: there Melchizedek honored Abraham (Gen 14), there Abraham was willing to sacrifice Isaac (Gen 22). Joseph's story reminds Israel of how God works in unseen ways, through human decisions, and how God somehow makes all things work together for good for his people, as God did in the events that brought Solomon to the throne.

The third situation with which we can connect Genesis is the exile. In this time of disaster Genesis brings a similar message to that of the prophets of that time, such as Ezekiel (see chap. 10 below). It asserts that God is a God of grace, and it thus suggests that all is not lost when we fail: God can still be faithful. It emphasizes the unearned goodness of God expressed in the initial creation. It asserts the continuing faithfulness of God at the time of the flood—disaster may come, but it is not God's last word. It reminds Israel that God's promises to Abraham were given before Abraham did anything to earn God's favor. It is this point in Genesis that Paul appeals to (Rom 4). All Abraham did was believe God's promise—he was treated as God's man on the strength of just that. Now, in the exile, the story suggests, you are challenged to believe God's promise again.

The point is made in Genesis by describing the covenants God made with Noah (Gen 9) and Abraham (Gen 15). God's covenant relationship with people did not begin at the exodus (when the instructions about lifestyle were given) but much earlier (before there were any instructions to obey). This relationship is one of grace. It stems simply from God's goodness.

The relationship between Genesis and the exile appears in the particular practices that the stories mention. In exile and in dispersion the distinctive outward marks of a Jew have always been important: the Jewish people are people who observe the sabbath, who keep the basic kosher law (avoiding consuming blood by draining it from an animal when it is killed), and whose males are circumcised. In exile the challenge is to be willing to stand out by such practices.

Genesis helps the exiles to meet this challenge by asserting that these practices have an authority even greater than the Mosaic law. Circumcision goes back to Abraham (Gen 17). The kosher law goes back to Noah (Gen 9:4). And the sabbath goes back to the pattern of God's own activity at creation: God did his week's work and then rested (Gen 2:2). The importance of these marks of Israel is thus heavily underlined.

These stories thus relate to periods in Israel's life, which helps to short-circuit the problems that arise when they are treated as scientific narratives. There are various ways of fitting scientific discoveries and the creation stories together. But we miss the point of Genesis if we concentrate on this question. Genesis is concerned to bring a message to people in its day that will help them to understand their own lives and help them to follow the truth. Its question in not whether the world was created in six days or not, but rather, whether the world was created in a purposeful way at all. Or was it the result of bickering among the gods, as the Babylonians thought? Or was it just an accident, as modern scientists have to believe if they do not believe in God? Genesis asserts that the world was planned by someone, that it belongs to someone, and that this someone thought it was good.

THE PROMISE TO ISRAEL'S ANCESTORS
(GENESIS 12–50)

So the story of the world leads into the story of one family, the ancestors of Israel. (They used to be regularly referred to as the patriarchs, but this word covers only the men—and "patriarchal" is often now a negative idea.) Abraham's clan is summoned from Mesopotamia to Canaan. The key passage that sets the scene for the whole is God's summons to Abraham:

> Leave your native land, your relatives, and your father's home, and go to a country that I am going to show you. I will give you many descendants, and they will become a great nation. I will bless you and make your name famous, so that you will be a blessing. I will bless people who bless you, but I will curse people who curse you. And through you I will bless all the nations. (Gen 12:1-3)

The promise is restated several times in Genesis, and the lives of Abraham and Sarah, Isaac and Rebekah, and Jacob and his family illustrate how it is fulfilled in part in their lifetimes. These stories also show how the promise is often in danger of not being fulfilled. Israel's ancestors are not plastic heroes but real people who are chosen by God but make human-size mistakes and ever threaten to lose what they hope to gain.

It is worth looking at these chapters, too, against the three backgrounds noted earlier (the exodus, David and Solomon, and the exile). First, the promise of a land leads directly to the story of the Israelites' exodus from Egypt. The promise that inspired Moses was that "the God of the ancestors" was now fulfilling his undertaking to give his people a permanent home in Canaan (Ex 3). And when the Israelites had escaped from Egypt, they invaded the land of Canaan under Joshua in the conviction that God had already promised to give it to them (Josh 1). At the end of their campaigns Joshua was able to testify that "Yahweh your God has given you all the good things that he promised. Every promise he made has been kept; not one has failed" (Josh 23:14).

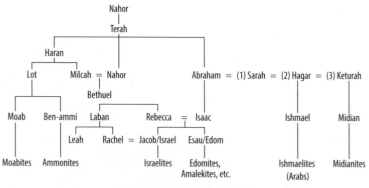

The Sons of Jacob (the heads of the Israelite tribes)
By Leah – Reuben, Simeon, Levi, Judah, Issachar, Zebulum
By Rachel's maid, Bilhah – Dan, Naphtali
By Leah's maid, Zilpah – Gad, Asher
By Rachel – Joseph, Benjamin
In this geneology, children are not necessarily listed in order of age (e.g., Jacob was younger than Esau).

Figure 4.1. The family of Abraham

The theme of promise and fulfillment runs through the opening books of the Bible. God promises Abraham's family that he will make them a great nation, make his own covenant with them, and give them a land of their own (Gen 17). This promise is reasserted several times in Genesis, but the book sees little evidence of its fulfillment. The family grows but still numbers less than a hundred. They wander about in the land of Canaan but have to leave it again. They hear God speak and they worship him, yet they seem to live no closer to him and to make no less of a mess of their life than do families to whom God has not spoken as he had to them.

The New Testament writers were to believe that "the promise to Abraham" was fulfilled through Christ; it is to him that the Old Testament promise looks forward. But within the Old Testament, the promise to Abraham begins to be fulfilled when the Israelites escape from Egypt.

THE EXODUS STORY (EXODUS 1–18)

The books of Exodus, Leviticus, and Numbers take Israel from bondage in Egypt to meeting God at Mount Sinai, and then on to the edge of the Promised Land. The books tell one continuous story; they are not three separate books. While it is possible to divide the story into episodes, the natural breaks do not come at the end of Exodus and the end of Leviticus (as table 4.2 shows).

Exodus begins with the first stage of God's promise already fulfilled: the family has become a people. The rest of the promise seems a long way away. They are enslaved and demoralized. It is not surprising that oppressed peoples today, such as African Americans and Majority World nations, have been able to identify with Israel in Egypt. The story of their oppression has a modern ring.

What brings Israel out of Egypt is something very unmodern. It is the hand of God. God declares that he is going to fulfill his promise and thus reveal himself in a new way, as Yahweh (Jehovah in the old translations), which means something like "the God who is there and makes his presence felt."

God gives this undertaking to an Israelite named Moses, who had narrowly escaped death as a child and had then been brought up in the Egyptian court. Moses now clearly takes the nonelites' side and challenges the king of Egypt to release the Israelites to go and hold a religious festival in their God's honor. Moses is the means of various chastisements that seek to persuade the king to let the Israelites go, but the Egyptians continue to resist until their eldest sons are killed and their army is destroyed at the Reed Sea (not what we refer to as the Red Sea but an area of marsh, probably in the region of the Suez Canal).

The story is dramatic and bloody. It is typical of the way the Bible describes the real world, a world like the one we see portrayed on the television news. Exodus declares that Israel's God involved himself in this world and proved that he was God and that the king and the gods of Egypt were not. He could beat them at their own game.

The triumph of the exodus became a central feature in Israel's thinking. It had proved that God was with them. It was the basis of the demands he made on their lives. And it suggested the way they hoped he would act in their lives in the future, when they would experience a new exodus (especially in the time of the renewed bondage of the exile). It was even supposed to be the basis of a change in the way they reckoned time: they were to make the festival of Passover (when God "passed over" the Israelites at the time of his judgment on the Egyptians [see Ex 12]) the beginning of their year from now on. It would be especially at the Passover festival that they told the exodus story, and thus preserved and developed the narrative we now have in Exodus.

An important feature of the Israelites' faith was their knowledge that their God was working out a purpose in their history. Other nations also assumed that their gods were involved in their national fortunes. If things went wrong, the deity must be displeased for some reason (people tend to make the same assumption today). Israel's assumptions about God and history were more deeply thought out. Its story was not a chapter of accidents but one in which God was involved from start to finish, in the big events and the everyday routine. He was not just the one who started the world going, or even just the power behind nature, nor was he only interested in people's religious observances. He was the God behind the events in the newspapers.

Although his purpose in all those events cannot necessarily be seen straightaway (unless there is a prophet to tell us what it is), there *is* a purpose at work in them.

This basic conviction of Israel goes back to the story of the exodus, when God first involved himself in the nation's history and rescued the oppressed people from its affliction.

ISRAEL AT MOUNT SINAI (EXODUS 19–NUMBERS 10)

After the excitement of the exodus story, the account of Israel's two-month stay near Mount Sinai can seem tedious, and readers of the Bible can get stuck here. At a first reading, it is worth simply following the basic story outline of the making, breaking, and remaking of the "covenant" (see table 4.2). The bulk of the rest of the chapters (the second column on the table) concerns the setting up of Israel's fundamental religious institutions—the sanctuary tent, the priesthood, and the holy camp. The remainder is made up of collections of instructions that relate to Israel's religious life. Most of this material we shall deal with in chapter nine, on Israel's rule of life. What is worth noting here is that the instructions don't appear on their own but only in the context of the story. As I have noted, *torah* embraces both story and law.

The content of God's instructions is similar to the instructions about lifestyle accepted by other Middle Eastern peoples. But these instructions appear in a distinctive context in the Old Testament because they are linked with the story of what God did for Israel. There are several ways of understanding this link, and all may be appropriate at different points. The Ten Commandments (Ex 20) begin, "I am Yahweh your God who brought you out of Egypt, where you were serfs. Worship no God but me.

Do not make for yourselves images." God implies that his act of rescuing Israel gives him the right to lay down how Israel should live. He has shown himself to be one who is faithful to people; therefore Israelites are to be faithful to one another. He has shown himself to be holy; therefore Israel is to be holy.

A stress on living as God expects could seem a burden, as it is sometimes seen in the New Testament, but Jews have not seen it that way. Two other ways of linking faith and obedience help. One is that Israel saw God's instructions as his gracious gift to Israel. It was not a collection of limitations imposed by God, but a body of guidance to lead God's people in the best way. Bringing the Israelites out of Egypt and giving them his instructions are both the outworking of his grace. The other is to see the obeying of God's instructions as the grateful and appropriate response that God's people give to what he has done on his people's behalf. We shall examine this insight when we look at Deuteronomy.

A surprising feature at the heart of the story of Israel's time at Sinai is the account of the breaking and remaking of the covenant. Hardly had Moses disappeared up Mount Sinai when Israel indulged in the making of an image, which was forbidden by the Ten Commandments—not the worship of a different god but the representation of Yahweh by means of something humanly created (Ex 32). God stopped short of destroying the whole people for this act, but the story makes clear that the sin of the Garden of Eden (where human beings immediately broke the one prohibition God gave them) is going to characterize the story of the people of God too. Israel is only a nation of human beings.

Table 4.2. Exodus 16–Numbers 10

The main story: the making of the covenant	The forming of the congregation of Yahweh	Sections of instruction
Exodus 16–24: the giving of the instructions	Exodus 25–31: instructions for the sacred tent and priesthood	
Exodus 32–34: the people's rebellion and restoration	Exodus 35–40: building of the sacred tent	Leviticus 1–7: Rules for sacrifice
	Leviticus 8–10: institution of priesthood	Leviticus 11–15: Rules about uncleanness
	Leviticus 16: Provision for atonement	Leviticus 17–27: Rules about holiness
	Numbers 1–10: Preparations for the march	
(On to Numbers 10 for the main story continuing as Israel leaves Sinai)		

THE JOURNEY TO THE EDGE OF THE PROMISED LAND (NUMBERS 11–36)

The motif of rebellion that we meet in the Sinai story runs through this next section. Even before the Israelites reached Sinai, they had doubted the goodwill and the power of Moses and God (Ex 15–17). This note dominates the book of Numbers. In effect it constitutes a turning back on the purpose for which God had called Israel. The people wish they had never left Egypt. God declares that, because of their unfaith, the whole generation will be prevented from entering the Promised Land (Num 14), and so for a generation the people live a nomadic life in the northern part of the Sinai Peninsula and the Negev. There was nothing inherently dangerous or unusual about this. Other peoples lived nomadic lives in this area, then as now. But it was a chastisement for Israel in that it meant a delay in the fulfillment of God's promise to give them a land.

As Israel reached the edge of the Promised Land, they met up with "Balaam the son of Beor" (Num 22–24). Here the theme of blessing and cursing, which appeared in Genesis in connection with the giving of God's promise, reappears near the end of Genesis–Numbers, as the fulfillment of the promise draws near. Balaam was hired to curse Israel and thus to bring trouble upon it. But he finds that he is able only to bless them—to promise that they will enjoy power and prosperity. As God had once declared to Abraham, Balaam declares "whoever blesses Israel will be blessed" (Num 24:9). As we have noted in connection with Genesis, such a story would have spoken powerfully not only to the exodus generation but also to those who lived (for instance) in the time of Solomon, when the promise of blessing was most clearly fulfilled, and in the exile, when Israel lived again only on the edge of the Promised Land and in need of God to fulfill his promise of blessing once more.

4

FROM TRIUMPH
TO DEFEAT

Deuteronomy to Kings

ALTHOUGH DEUTERONOMY BELONGS TO THE TORAH, it also looks forward to Joshua, Judges, Samuel, and Kings. Deuteronomy gives Israel the basis for its life in Canaan; the books that follow Deuteronomy describe how Israel entered the land but in the end failed to cope with the problems it met there because it failed to take Deuteronomy's teaching seriously.

The final version that we have of the books from Deuteronomy to Kings must belong to the exile (or later), which is where the story leaves off in 2 Kings. But the books include much material belonging to earlier centuries. As with Genesis to Numbers, then, these books can be read at several levels. They tell us about the times to which they refer, and also about the faith of the period in which they were written.

DEUTERONOMY

Deuteronomy is Moses' last speech before his death just the other side of the Jordan. It is really more of a sermon than a speech; it is full of exhortations to take God seriously. Moses keeps urging, "Listen, Israel, to the statutes and ordinances that I speak in your hearing this day; you shall learn them, and take care to do them"; "Love Yahweh your God, and keep his commandments always."

More clearly than any other part of the Bible, Deuteronomy portrays the relationship between God and his people in the light of the relationship between a great king and his subject peoples. We know something of this relationship from the political treaties of the day. In these, the great king reminds his underlings of how relationships between them have been in the past; he describes the attitude of loyalty he expects in the future and may make specific requirements about the conducting of their affairs; and he reminds them of the consequences, good and bad, that will follow from loyalty or disloyalty.

Moses' sermon in Deuteronomy follows this pattern:

1–3	Reminder of the past relationship
4–11	The attitude God requires now
12–26	God's specific requirements (These laws are much longer than one would expect in a document based on a treaty. Deuteronomy is influenced by Middle Eastern law codes as well as by treaties.)
27–28	The consequences that will follow
29–33	Closing words (These include some further features reminiscent of the treaties, such as the writing down of the document and its placing in the temple.)

We will look at the detailed requirements in chapter nine. It is worth noting here that the first of them, which required Israel to worship only in the place that Yahweh chose, was of key significance in the reform of Judah's last faithful king, Josiah. This reform included the implementation of what was required by a Torah book found in the temple store in Jerusalem (2 Kings 22), and this Torah book was apparently some form of what we call Deuteronomy. The influence of the Deuteronomic approach to things can be seen also in the book of Jeremiah (who also lived in this period) and in the books of Kings themselves (which were completed soon after). The distinctive phrases and emphases of Deuteronomy also appear there.

The importance of worshiping only where God chose lay in the concern shared by all these books for loyalty to the God of Israel. There were places of worship all over Canaan, and it was natural for Israelites who lived in different parts of the land to worship at these. But the origin of these sanctuaries lay in the religion of the Canaanites, with its concern with fertility and its worship of Baal. It was difficult for the Israelites to avoid being influenced by this religion, and Deuteronomy seeks to guard against it. Loyalty to Yahweh is of fundamental significance. Josiah took "the place that Yahweh chooses" to be Jerusalem, though Deuteronomy itself (with its setting beyond the Jordan) does not say it is.

JOSHUA

The book of Joshua is the story of Joshua. It begins with his challenge to Israel at the beginning of his period of leadership, as Israel still waits encamped the other side of the Jordan. It ends with his challenge to Israel at the end of his life, as Israel begins its settled life west of the Jordan. In between these two gatherings, the first half of the book describes how Joshua led Israel in its conquest of the land, and the second half tells how he distributed the land among the Israelite clans.

1	Initial challenge
2–12	Conquest of the land
13–22	Distribution of the land
23–24	Closing challenge

Following the Torah, the book of Joshua tells how the plan of God was finally accomplished. The undertaking that God had made back in Abraham's day is fulfilled; the purpose God initiated through Moses is completed. "Not one thing has failed of all the good things that Yahweh your God promised concerning you" (Josh 23:14).

As we find with some other books, however, within this united structure of the book of Joshua very diverse material is included. There are the speeches, which express the teaching of Deuteronomy and challenge Israel to obey God both as it conquers the land and in its life there. There are the tales of the spies and Rahab (Josh 2), the capture of Jericho (Josh 6), the sin of Achan at Ai (Josh 7–8), the cleverness of the Gibeonites (Josh 9), and the slaughter of the kings on the day the sun stood still (Josh 10). There are the more terse notes of the military statistics of Joshua's campaigns. There are detailed records regarding which village was to belong to whom. The variety of material in this book opens the door on the variety of Israel's life, the different contexts in which the material that eventually made up the Bible was preserved (the sanctuary, the campfire, the records office), and the variety of significance that the material must have had for the Israelites (exhortation, entertainment, historical interest, legal need).

As part of Genesis–Kings, however, the book of Joshua was finalized in the exile, and in this context its message is clear.

Israel is once again outside its Promised Land, but the book reminds it that the land was won at the first by God's gift—so God could make it possible for Israel to gain it again. The land had been distributed among the clans at the God's bidding—it belonged to him, and he could give it to them again. The challenge to them was to respond to Joshua's challenge to take God's instructions seriously.

Stressing that the land was given by God, the major part of the book emphasizes one side of the story of how Israel came to possess it. It is aware, however, that there were other aspects to the story than the glorious conquest. The final chapter, with its challenge to an apparently mixed audience to make up their minds to serve God, hints that many of the later "Israelites" had lived in the land before the conquest and now joined the invaders who were perhaps their relatives. The opening chapter of the next book adds another dimension to the picture of the process whereby the land came to belong to Israel.

JUDGES–1 SAMUEL 7

The excitement of the book of Joshua is followed by a telling footnote, which is now the introduction to the book of Judges. We could have inferred from Joshua that the conquest was gloriously consummated. But from time to time the book notes that Israel's occupation of the land was far from complete, and now we learn more about the areas that were not conquered. They were actually the most difficult ones, areas where the more sophisticated Canaanites were concentrated. There thus remains a challenge before Israel: to enter fully into the possession God has given them, to mop up the not insignificant remains of the Canaanites.

Instead, the story in Judges has to relate a series of disasters, all following a similar pattern. The pattern is announced by Judges 2–3:

1. The Israelites become unfaithful to God.

2. God is angry with them and allows them to be oppressed by enemies.

3. In response to their pleas for help God raises up a "judge" or deliverer to defeat their enemies.

4. The land has rest until the Israelites rebel against God again.

The stories that follow introduce us to figures such as Deborah (Judg 4–5), Gideon (Judg 6–8), and Samson (Judg 13–16). The stories recount events that happened to different clans in different parts of the land over a period of two centuries from Joshua to Saul. The book as a whole casts them into the framework of the pattern previously described, seeing them all as events in the life of the whole people of God.

The scene is increasingly one of moral, religious, and political anarchy, and the later chapters make clear that they understand the problem to be the fact that "everyone did just as they pleased" because "there was no king in Israel at that time" (Judg 21:25). The book thus prepares the way for the institution of the monarchy in 1 Samuel. The first chapters of 1 Samuel essentially belong to the judges sequence. The oppression of the Philistines, which leads to Saul's taking office, is the last and most awful example of the cycle of sin and tragedy that runs through Judges.

We may again see the composition of this book as a whole as designed to speak to the people in exile. Here they have fallen into the deepest sin (1) and experienced the deepest affliction (2). But perhaps the pattern can be completed again: if they turn back to God he may restore them (3), and they may once again enjoy rest in the land (4).

1 SAMUEL 8–1 KINGS 11

The story from Joshua to 2 Kings is a continuous one, and any subdivisions, whether those made in the present form of the biblical text itself or the alternatives I suggest here, need to be seen as marking the "chapters" of a longer whole. As we have seen, the beginning of 1 Samuel describes the final and greatest of the crises of the period of the judges. Again the people sin, again God punishes, again they pray, again God restores: but now a new "chapter" begins, because the one through whom the answer comes is not merely a judge but a king.

Kings will be a mixed blessing, and the ambiguity of the institution of the monarchy is reflected in the story of its origin. The story so far has prepared us to see kings as a good thing, because the alternative is the ever deeper chaos of the period of the judges. Yet God is supposed to be Israel's king, so the request for a human monarch is a rejection of him. This attitude appears also in the earlier chapters of Judges: Gideon, for instance, refuses to be made king (Judg 8:23).

Only three kings ruled over the united nation. Each begins as a hero but ends as a tragedy. Saul wins some splendid victories but is immediately involved in the tension that is to bedevil many kings. On the one hand, he must exercise powerful leadership and do what the situation demands. On the other, he must obey God, especially in what God says through his prophets. Because Saul gives priority to the former, he is rejected and soon begins to show symptoms of psychosis in his attitude to his general David, whose achievements and popularity threaten to eclipse his king's. Saul dies a lonely and tragic figure, defeated by his enemies and alienated from his God as well as from former associates such as Samuel and David.

David has already taken over the status of the hero of the story before he comes to the throne. If the story goes back to David's reign, it is not surprising that he is the hero, but a remarkable feature of the portrait of David is its ambiguity. Is he the man with an eye for the main chance, the man who falls on his feet? Or the man who seeks to go God's way, the man God consequently blesses? The story can be read both ways. What is indisputable is the military achievement of David in disposing of the Philistine threat once and for all, and in building the biggest empire Israel ever knew.

The tragedy of David, as the later chapters of 2 Samuel show, was that his gifts as a general were not matched by wisdom in personal and family relationships. These chapters reveal a story of sin and incompetence that is only too human. And yet, the story implies, God's providence is able to achieve what God wanted through it all: Solomon becomes king.

Solomon's story, too, begins with his achievement: supremely, the building of a temple for God, though also other buildings in Jerusalem and elsewhere, and the consolidation and organization of the empire inherited from David. The tragedy of Solomon was that "he loved many foreign women" (1 Kings 11): the sin is not the polygamy but the opening of the door to the influence of alien religions in Israel. Kings sees this as the key to the downfall of Israel's state in the short and the long term.

1 KINGS 12–2 KINGS 25

After Solomon, the books of Kings tell the complicated, interwoven story of the two kingdoms of Ephraim and Judah until the national existence of both came to an end. The major question posed by the books from Joshua to Kings—why did Ephraim and Judah fall?—is now in the forefront of the presentation. The answer is that, by and large, the kings of Ephraim and Judah failed to lead their peoples in the ways of David, who for all his personal faults is a paradigm of faithfulness to God. In contrast, they repeatedly encouraged Ephraim and Judah to follow the Baals, the gods of the Canaanites, who were worshiped at sanctuaries all over the country.

The pattern of the books is to introduce each king with his date, his family background, and a general judgment on his reign, then sometimes to relate particular events from his reign, then to tell of his death and who succeeded him. Second Kings 12, the story of Joash, provides a straightforward example of the pattern.

Several of the kings are regarded as particularly significant. Ephraim's first king, Jeroboam, is the archetypal villain. He first set his country on the wrong road by taking it away from the worship of Yahweh in Jerusalem (1 Kings 12–13), and it is because Ephraim followed his way that it was cast off (2 Kings 17). Judah's equivalent to Jeroboam is Manasseh (2 Kings 21), Judah's archetypal villain, who is blamed for the final fall of Judah (2 Kings 24).

On either side of Manasseh are described the only two kings who are assessed very positively, Hezekiah (2 Kings 18–20) and Josiah (2 Kings 22–23). These uniquely did what was pleasing to God and walked in the ways of David, but they were not able to avert the fate toward which kings such as Manasseh were hurrying the nation.

As well as emphasizing the kings' responsibility as those who led their people in the right or the wrong way, and the importance of loyalty to Jerusalem, its temple, and its worship as a criterion of true religion, Kings stresses the role of prophets in the story of the two kingdoms. Kings gives many chapters to the stories of Elijah and Elisha, and at other key points introduces a prophet who brings God's word to a situation and thus is either the means of God blessing his people or, more often, of bringing a warning of judgment.

Overall, the books of Kings tell a gloomy story. Yet in the exile they offer glimmers of hope. The reforms of Hezekiah and Josiah had not been ignored by God—God honors those who turn to him. It might still be so. God had committed himself to the line of David: he might still concern himself with David's people. Indeed the last paragraph of the books tells of the release of a potential heir to David's throne, who had been imprisoned in Babylon, so that it hints that, despite the gloominess of the story, God may not yet have finished with Israel.

5

THE STORY
OF THE COMMUNITY

Chronicles, Ezra, and Nehemiah

WITH 1 CHRONICLES WE FIND OURSELVES back where we started, with Adam; 1–2 Chronicles retell the story from Genesis to Kings.

They tell the story from a different perspective, however. In some ways it is only a sharpened version of the perspective of Kings, for one important theme of Kings is Jerusalem and the temple, and these are even more central in Chronicles. In fact, nearly everything that does not directly deal with Jerusalem and the temple is omitted.

Thus the whole history up to Saul is compressed into eight introductory chapters of genealogies. The real story begins with David, who planned the temple, and Solomon, who built it. In their reigns, anything that merely concerned their private lives or their political activities is omitted as irrelevant. What concerns the temple and its worship is retained and expanded. After David and Solomon, the history of Ephraim is quietly and totally omitted. When the northern clans cut themselves off from Jerusalem, they cut themselves off from the story of God's people.

Even the great stories of Elijah and Elisha disappear because of the authors' desire to concentrate on this chosen theme.

A comparison of Chronicles and Samuel-Kings shows that it not only covers the same ground. The author took much of the material from the earlier work (or from some other version of the story that is now lost). Whole sections in Chronicles follow the text of Samuel-Kings. Some have additions made to them. Other whole sections, as I have noted, are quite omitted: they are irrelevant to the message the author wants to bring. They are in effect replaced by extra material on the life of kings such as David, Hezekiah, and Josiah. Many of these extra stories are dramatic accounts of famous victories in war, won against great odds.

Often the only sections from Chronicles that we read (for instance, in church lectionary or Bible study schemes) are the ones that supplement Samuel-Kings, and then only the interesting ones. But the books as a whole deserve to be read in their own right. They have a clear message relating to the different period in which they were written.

Kings, written in the exile, admits Israel's sin and perhaps hints at the hope that it might one day be restored again. But when this restoration came a few years later, Israel did not regain its political freedom. It was now more like a religious community under foreign overlords, rather as Jews have been in Europe. So the temple and its worship were even more central to its faith than they had been before the exile, and Chronicles was written to tell the story of the temple for people for whom it was all-important.

The story continues in Ezra, which describes how the temple was rebuilt and its worship reconstituted. In this sense the books of Ezra and Nehemiah are a continuation of the books of Chronicles, though it may be that they came first and Chronicles was written as their prequel. After describing the restoration of the temple, in the century before Ezra and Nehemiah's own day, they tell how the life of the community in Jerusalem was reordered under the leadership of Ezra and Nehemiah, as emissaries from the Persian court.

There are now no kings descended from David whose story can be told; there were no Davidic kings after the exile. The compiler of Chronicles is interested in David not because there were Davidic kings in his day, nor because he is looking forward to a day when there will once again be a king on David's throne, but because it was David who laid the plans and made the provisions for the temple, which is now the heart of the life of God's people. God has fulfilled his promises, not indeed by giving his people political independence again but by returning to the temple that he had left because of his people's sin. So Chronicles goes into detail in connection with the temple, dwelling on its planning by David (1 Chron 21–29), its building by Solomon (2 Chron 2–7), and the various reforms of its worship (Hezekiah, 2 Chron 29–31; Josiah, 2 Chron 34–35). The account in Ezra 1–6 of the restoration of the Judahites from exile centers on the rebuilding of the temple. Cyrus commanded the Judahites to return for this purpose (Ezra 1), the first act of the people who returned was to recommence worship in the broken-down building and to initiate rebuilding (Ezra 3), and the story of the return comes to a triumphant and joyful climax with the completion of this project (Ezra 5–6). The temple is the very life center of the people.

Chronicles naturally concerns itself with the worship offered in the temple and often notes in detail how worship rules were kept. It describes the various ministries exercised in the temple. Naturally the priests, with their important responsibility in offering sacrifice, are prominent. More striking is the frequent mention of the Levites (the priests' assistants)—some scholars have inferred that the writer must have been a Levite himself! They are the leaders of worship and singing in the temple; Chronicles emphasizes the joyful praise of Israel's worship, which is the very heart of what it means to be the people of God. Striking, too, is the frequent appearance of prophets in the Chronicler's picture of the temple worship. If they are critical of Israel's worship, it is from within the institution, rather than from outside it: they urge the congregation to order their worship aright.

As we have noted, Ephraim loses its place in the history of the people of God, because it cut itself off from David, from Jerusalem, and from the temple. Nevertheless, the door remains open to Ephraim to return, and the door is also open to foreigners to be involved in the service of God. At the same time, the overall emphasis of Ezra-Nehemiah in particular is to be wary of alien influence. One feature of the life of the times was the danger that the Judahites would lose their identity and become indistinguishable from other peoples in the area. The books of Ezra and Nehemiah speak of other people who wanted to join in the rebuilding of the temple, and of mixed marriages between Judahites and people such as Ammonites and Moabites. The books take a hard line on these issues out of their concern that the people of God should not lose their purity and their distinctiveness.

So God's people, as Chronicles-Ezra-Nehemiah see them, are in a privileged but an insecure position. The books' thrust is thus to emphasize that the people are called to trust and obey God. In story and sermon, the books keep reminding them of the characteristics of God that ought to stimulate them to this life of faith. He is the mighty God who makes it possible for his people to win battles against impossible odds, the just God who honors those who honor him but sees that the wicked get their deserts, the faithful God who fulfills his word, the gracious God who forgives and restores those who return to him. So people can afford to trust him, and cannot afford not to obey him, in their everyday lives.

Table 6.1. Chronicles–Ezra–Nehemiah

Introduction 1 Chronicles 1–9	David, who planned the temple 1 Chronicles 10–29	The return and the rebuilding of the temple Ezra 1–6	
	Solomon, who built the temple 2 Chronicles 1–9	The arrival and reforms of Ezra and Nehemiah Ezra 7–10; Nehemiah 8–10	Nehemiah's testimony: rebuilding and reform Nehemiah 1–7; 11–13
	The story up to the exile 2 Chronicles 10–36		

6

SHORT STORIES

Ruth, Esther, Jonah, and Daniel

WITHIN THE BOOKS WE HAVE ALREADY considered are sections of story that maybe once existed on their own. Among these are the stories of Joseph (in Genesis), of how Solomon came to succeed to the throne (in Samuel-Kings), and of Nehemiah (in the book of Nehemiah). Other stories were not incorporated into the great history works but stand on their own.

RUTH

The book of Ruth is the tale of a Moabite girl who marries into an Israelite family who were staying in Moab (east of the Jordan) during a famine. After the tragic death of her husband and her father-in-law, Ruth accompanies her mother-in-law, Naomi, back to the family hometown, Bethlehem. There she wins the love of another man from Naomi's family, Boaz, who marries her and brings comfort to Naomi as the couple present her with a grandchild, reestablishing the position of the family and its land.

That bald summary of the story's plot may hint at how charming a story it is in its own right, before we begin to ask why it is in the Bible. It illustrates how God works through unexpected and ordinary people. It takes a notably open attitude to its foreign heroine, which contrasts with the attitude taken by Ezra and Nehemiah to people such as the Moabites when (unlike Ruth) they don't commit themselves to Israel and its God. The openness is the more remarkable when we reach the final punch line of the story in the closing paragraph. The son of Ruth and Boaz turns out to be grandfather of King David: a worthy reward for the courage and loyalty of Ruth, and the chivalry of Boaz.

JONAH

The story of Jonah is set two or three centuries later, in the time of the Ephraimite kingdom. His book appears among the Twelve Prophets (see chap. 10). God commissions him to go and preach to the great Assyrian city of Nineveh. Not warming to this calling, he catches a ship going in the opposite direction but finds he cannot so easily escape God, who sends a storm after him. To rescue the ship from God's anger, Jonah lets himself be thrown overboard; to rescue Jonah from the sea, God sends a fish to catch him and take him back to land. Having learned his lesson, Jonah proceeds to Nineveh. To his disgust he convinces the Ninevites that they should repent and avoid God's judgment. The final scene pictures Jonah's further disgust at God's permitting the death of a tree that had given him shade; God points out that his concern for the tree makes a strange contrast with his lack of concern for the Ninevites.

If the charm of Ruth is evident from the plot, the humor of Jonah will be clear from this outline. Jonah is, at point after point, an illustration of how not to be a prophet. In particular, like Ruth, the book suggests that God often has a much more positive attitude to those who do not (yet) belong to his people than the attitude those people themselves have.

ESTHER

Our third short story is a grimmer tale. The scene is the court of the Persian king Artaxerxes. The king's prime minister, Haman, persuades him to authorize the elimination of the Jewish population of the empire, and many of the Persian peoples prepare to implement the order. But one of the king's wives, Esther, happens to be Jewish, while her foster-father, Mordecai, had once rescued the king from assassination. These two are able to get the tables turned in the nick of time. Haman is hanged on the gallows he prepared for Mordecai, and the Jews slaughter the people who attack them.

The bloody story epitomizes the Jewish people's awareness about their own history. Often blood has been shed, usually theirs. But the story shows how sometimes God is in control behind the scenes even though you can't see him (the book does not actually mention him), working out a just purpose though "chance" and through the selfish decisions of human beings.

DANIEL

Daniel and his friends were young men transported to Babylon at the time of the exile. Two themes recur in the stories about them. The first is the religious challenge brought to them by having to live in a foreign environment. Will they keep up their distinctive way of life? Will they bow down to idols? Will they pray to the emperor? Their faithfulness in these matters leads to sentences that they will be burned to death or eaten alive. But God is faithful to them, as they have been to him.

The stories' second theme is the young men's wisdom. Babylon was a renowned intellectual center, but it turns out that Daniel and his friends can outdo the great minds of Babylon because of the insight their God gives them. In particular, Daniel can interpret the meaning of some disturbing dreams that the king has; on top of this, he receives significant visions himself. The second half of the book concentrates on these visions. (We will look at them in chap. 12.)

So the stories challenge their hearers to be faithful to God and his teaching, and to trust that he is the Lord of the secrets of world history.

7

THE STORY OF JESUS AND THE CHURCH

Matthew to Acts

A GOSPEL IS A UNIQUE FORM OF WRITING to tell a unique kind of story. The Christian church centered its faith on a man, Jesus, who lived thirty-something years. But all that was important about him (his achievements and teaching) belong to his last three years, so they concentrate on these. And what really mattered most about him was the way his story ended: so the Gospels give a third of their attention to the very last days of his life.

The four Gospels are named after men we hear about in the New Testament itself. Matthew and John were among Jesus' twelve closest disciples, and Mark and Luke were involved in events in the early history of the church described in the Acts of the Apostles. But the four names do not come in the Gospels themselves, only in the headings ("According to Matthew," etc.), which were added later. So we can't be sure whether these men were the authors of the books credited to them, though there are no more plausible candidates for the role.

The Gospels were written within a few decades of the death of Jesus, maybe between AD 65 and 100. Luke and John tell us why they wrote, and it is not unlikely that the same concerns provided at least part of Matthew and Mark's motivation. They wrote so that people could have reliable information on the course of Jesus' ministry and on the content of his teaching, so that they could have a secure foundation for faith in him (see Lk 1:1-4; Jn 20:30-31).

The Gospels are not exactly biographies of Jesus. They do not describe his appearance or personality, and their treatment of most of his life is sketchy. Nor do we have significant further information about him from outside the New Testament. Certain facts about him—that he lived, exercised a public ministry, died in the time of Pontius Pilate, and soon came to be worshiped all over the eastern Mediterranean—are referred to by the first-century Jewish writer Josephus, by Jewish traditions preserved in the Talmud, or by Roman writers such as Pliny the Younger and Tacitus. In Christian writings outside the New Testament such as the so-called Gospel of Thomas, there are a few sayings that may go back to Jesus. But virtually our whole picture of his life, teaching, ministry, death, and resurrection comes from the Gospels in the New Testament.

The basic historical truth of the story of Jesus was essential to the truth of the Christian message, and it was the task of the apostles and others to give their eyewitness testimony to what they had seen and heard of Jesus. But people who could speak firsthand about Jesus' life and death and resurrection could not be everywhere, and must eventually die, so the eventual writing of the Gospels was important to the spread of the message about

Jesus. These writings give a fixed record of his story for people who had not known him.

Although all four Gospels are similar in outline, the first three resemble each other especially closely. They often repeat paragraphs in almost exactly the same words. That fact shows how these three *Synoptic* Gospels (the word means that they look at the story in the same way) are dependent on one another. It looks as if Mark came first, and as if his work has been used by Matthew and Luke. Matthew and Luke also have other material in common, which does not appear in Mark, and it looks as if this material comes from another earlier work that has not survived on its own, a collection of Jesus' teaching that is referred to as Q (from the German word *Quelle*, meaning "source"). There is a distinctive flavor about John's Gospel: we can't even be sure he had seen any of the others.

Thirty years or so separates Jesus' lifetime from the first written Gospels (though Q may have been written earlier), and as far as we know, during this time Jesus' story and teaching were passed on by word of mouth in the preaching and teaching of the church. No doubt this preaching and teaching dealt mostly with single sayings or incidents (as in our reading and preaching today), which means we can't be sure of putting all the individual events in their chronological order. But the period involved was short, and many who had heard and seen Jesus themselves were available to provide a check on the elaboration of the story. Thus, when writers such as Mark and Luke (who refers to the fact that he was not an eyewitness himself but made a point of gaining access to the testimony of those who were) came to produce their Gospels, there was no insuperable problem involved in providing their readers with reliable information.

Figure 7.1 at the end of this chapter describes the process whereby the Gospels may have come into existence.

The basic theme of the Gospels, particularly as the Synoptics put it, is that the coming of Jesus means that God is beginning to reign on earth. Jesus declares that "the time has come and the reign of God is near" (Mk 1:15). The phrase "reign of God" or "kingdom of God" does not refer to a particular place, like the United Kingdom. It describes God's ruling over the world as king. The Old Testament story has shown God reigning, but also how humanity resists God's reign. Committed Jews tried to make it a reality in their personal lives, but they also longed for a day when God would break into history again, vindicate his name, restore his people, punish his enemies, and fulfill his purpose. The idea of God's kingdom expressed some of the highest of their aspirations and some of the basic truths concerning God's purpose, and thus Jesus took it as his basic theme and let his life (and his death) correct any misunderstanding to which the phrase was open.

As the one who was bringing God's reign, Jesus spoke with an unprecedented authority. In fact, he taught with God's authority and invited people to learn from him the truth about God and God's ways. His authority proved itself over the power of illness, demon possession, natural forces, and the supernatural powers of evil that opposed the breaking in of God's reign. It won him varying degrees of allegiance from a wide variety of people—working people, agents of the Roman administration, social outcasts—though often their commitment was shallow, and Jesus made little impact on the religious leaders among his people.

The difficulty of getting through to many of these people led Jesus to speak in parables. A parable is not a simple, obvious illustration of a truth that is difficult to understand. It is almost the opposite: a story that is difficult to understand that relates to a truth that is easy enough to understand but hard to accept. Whoever heard of a boss paying the same wage no matter how many hours someone worked (Mt 20:1-16), or of killing the fatted calf for a renegade son while seeming to ignore his faithful brother (Lk 15:11-32)? In the parables, which show what God's reign is about, Jesus tells stories that begin in his listeners' everyday lives but contain a twist in the tail. He challenges them to puzzle out how the twist in the tail illustrates the surprising ways of God.

A recurrent theme here is the rejection of those who thought they were in a privileged position and the elevation of those who had no status at all. The reign of God is good news for people who need good news. But for people who are doing very well already, it is rather bad news, unless they can put themselves in the position of the despised outcast.

In the end, the Jewish leaders and the Gentile leaders collaborated to get rid of Jesus and got the ordinary people also to reject him. (The dynamics illustrate how this was not because the Jews were especially wicked—if Jesus came now, it would be those of us who are ministers and deacons and so on who would be most likely to be acting as the Jewish leaders did in Jesus' day.) Jesus' preaching of God's reign leads to his rejection and crucifixion, but that is only the beginning of another story.

Indeed, Jesus' rejection and death are not just an unforeseen calamity that is fortunately reversed by the resurrection. The day of Jesus' death came to be called Good Friday because his death was part of God's purpose and was not a hindrance to God ruling on earth but a means of God ruling on earth. Here were human beings and devils doing their worst, but even in letting them do their worst, Jesus won a victory over them. When Jesus on the cross said, "It's finished" (Jn 19:30), he meant not "I'm done" but "I've done it." There was nothing worse that we could do to God than kill his Son; he turned that action into something that could demonstrate his love and his power.

That achievement—and the life he lived before his death and resurrection—raises another question. Who is this man? It was a question people could hardly help asking. The popular answer of his followers was "He's the Messiah"—the Redeemer, the Davidic king God has promised the Jewish people. This was true, but misleading, because Jesus did not expect to become a king of Israel like David. Jesus referred to himself in terms of God's servant who accepts affliction on behalf of others (described in Is 42; 52–53), and of the Son of Man, the New Man, a triumphant but otherworldly figure. Beyond this, he manifests a uniquely close relationship with God as his Father, and John explicitly draws the inference that he is divine himself (just as I am human because my father is human). So John's Gospel begins by declaring that "the Word [the one through whom God expressed himself] became a human being" in Jesus (Jn 1:14), and ends by describing Thomas's acknowledgement of him as "My Lord and my God" (Jn 20:28).

The story of Jesus is the story of a conflict between him and the religious parties of his day, because he was threatening the status of the established leaders or competing with lesser groups for popular allegiance. Several groups are mentioned in the Gospels.

The *Sadducees* were the official priestly families. Their name indicates that they were the descendants of the original high priestly family of Zadok (the first high priest when the temple was built by Solomon). They were an establishment group. Theologically, they were conservative. They were deeply committed to the authority of the written Torah (the teaching of Moses). They did not accept the more detailed oral tradition that claimed to interpret what was written and to bring it up to date. They were suspicious of newer doctrines such as belief in angels and in the resurrection of the dead (see the story in Mk 12). They were also politically conservative: they were the aristocracy as well as the temple officials. They were the group closest to the political authorities (Herod and the Romans), on whom they depended for their position, and they tried to combine devotion to the law with political prudence.

The *Pharisees* were a kind of society, not a family group. Their name means "separated ones" and has its background in the rebellion against the Seleucids (see chap. 2), when the "pious ones" (*hasidim*) supported rebellion against these overlords who were trying to enforce Hellenistic practices on them. The Pharisees accepted a thoroughgoing commitment to keeping the Torah, including a wide range of oral teaching that regulated the detailed observance of requirements such as purity, tithing, and fasting. Their concern with purity is reflected in the discussion concerning matters such as hand-washing in Mark 7. It led to a determination to avoid too close contact with people who did not obey the Torah in such a careful way, who were therefore impure and liable to defile those who had contact with them. The Pharisees were not interested in political action but concentrated on piety in order to prepare for the breaking in of God's kingdom. They had strong hopes of the coming of the Messiah and of the resurrection of the dead.

The *Zealots* are not mentioned as a group in the Gospels. They became important in the context of events that led to the destruction of Jerusalem in AD 70, when they formed guerrilla bands in the Judahite hill country and were the driving force in the wars that led to the destruction of Jerusalem. They accepted the same theological beliefs as the Pharisees, but they were not satisfied with the view that the Jews simply had to wait until God brought about his reign. They believed they were called, like the rebels of the Maccabean time, to refuse to submit to the Roman emperor and to take the reins of history themselves.

The *Essenes* were a group who believed that God's people were called to separate themselves from ordinary society in a more radical way than the Pharisees. Their approach is seen in its most thoroughgoing form among those Jews who left Jerusalem to form their own community in the isolation of the desert shore of the Dead Sea at Qumran. They saw the temple's worship as corrupt and cut themselves off from it to prepare for God's own reestablishing of true worship. The New Testament makes no reference to the Essenes or to Qumran, but there are many parallels to their ideas and practices, such as baptism, the stress on repentance, the belief that they are the true people of God at the threshold of the messianic age, the emphasis on warfare against Satan, and the picture of a conflict between flesh and spirit and between light and darkness. The difference is that the followers of Jesus knew that the Messiah had come and knew who he was. What they had in common with the Essenes were the theological motifs used to express his significance.

The *scribes* or scholars, the teachers of Torah, are the final group who need to be mentioned. They are neither a family nor a society holding particular views but a set of people who might also be, for instance, Pharisees or believers in Jesus. They were theologians who had studied and could now offer teaching to others. They commissioned their own pupils to teach within their tradition: there were various schools and views. Jesus may thus be seen as a kind of scribe with his pupils (hence his being called "rabbi"), but there was something different about him. He taught not by reference to the teaching he had received from a master but on the basis of his own authority (see Mt 7:28-29).

The basic story in the Gospels, their fundamental picture of Jesus and his significance, is similar in all four accounts. But each has a distinctive slant and needs to be considered in its own right.

MARK

As far as we know, Mark was the first Gospel written, and it comes nearest to what we would have seen and heard if we had been present in Galilee or Jerusalem, watching and listening to Jesus.

Compared with the other Gospels, we are struck by its brevity. It begins where Jesus' ministry begins, and it has neither the background that Matthew and Luke provide in their family records and accounts of Jesus' birth and boyhood nor the elaborate theological introduction with which John prefaces his Gospel. Although it includes many examples of Jesus' teaching (including many of his parables), it has few of the longer discourses that are prominent, especially in Matthew and John. Its account of the resurrection is so succinct that it was soon felt to need supplementing by fuller accounts based on other Gospels (the extra "old endings" appended in our versions of the Gospel).

As you read Mark in its own right, several themes are striking. The earlier part of Jesus' ministry is characterized by two contrasting features. His authoritative ministry stirs up controversy and opposition among the Jewish leaders, but he quietly builds up a body of disciples through whom he plans to extend his work. The opposition increases, and even Jesus' family and home village reject him (Mk 6:1-4). He foresees that lynching looms over the story, but his disciples cannot acknowledge it (Mk 8:31-33; 9:30-32). Opponents and disciples coalesce as Jesus is betrayed and abandoned; at his death it is a Roman centurion who recognizes that he has stood in the presence of a son of God. Suddenly we are at the end of the story: Jesus has abandoned the tomb (though the event is not described) and is off to meet his disciples again in Galilee.

MATTHEW

A clear structure can be perceived in Matthew's Gospel: major sections of narrative and teaching alternate.

1–2	Introduction
3–4	The beginning of Jesus' ministry
5–7	His teaching of his disciples ("the Sermon on the Mount")
8–9	Healing miracles
10	His commission of the twelve disciples
11–12	Controversies
13	Parables about God's reign
14–17	The path toward the death (a)
18	Teaching on humility and forgiveness
19–22	The path toward the death (b)
23–25	Teaching on judgment
26–28	Death and resurrection

Matthew looks like a Gospel written for both Gentiles and Jews who have come to acknowledge Jesus as Messiah. It systematizes Jesus' teaching on the life of discipleship (especially in the Sermon on the Mount). While Matthew does not advocate that Jews must continue to observe the Torah and that Gentiles must also do so, he equally has no time for believers who do not see that their faith makes a difference to their lives. Mere enthusiastic worship, or even miracles done in Jesus' name, is not enough (Mt 7:21-27). This theme reappears in his treatment of the parables. To a greater degree than Mark he applies these to the life of the church. Whereas they originally addressed people confronted by Jesus' message in his lifetime, now they warn believers that they could fall into the same trap as those earlier Jews had done, if they do not remain faithful as they await the final coming of God's reign. Matthew closes his Gospel with the reminder that before that last day the good news about Jesus has to be preached to all nations, and if the church wants Jesus to be with them, they will find he is with them as they fulfill this commission.

Matthew shows his concern with the relationship of belief in Jesus to Jewish faith in two main ways. On the one hand, he emphasizes the failure of much of the Judaism of Jesus' day. Even the lives of the Pharisees and teachers of the Torah (who were very upright and faithful) were not good enough. It was these so-called leaders of Judaism who rejected the Jewish Messiah. On the other hand, he asserts that people who believe in Jesus are the true heirs to the Old Testament. He makes this point by his frequent references to the Old Testament, whose own goals are fulfilled in Jesus.

LUKE AND ACTS

In broad outline, Luke's Gospel, too, has a clear shape:

1–3	Introduction. Jesus' birth, his boyhood, and his baptism
4:1–9:50	His ministry in Galilee
9:51–19:27	His journey to Jerusalem
19:28–24:52	His final days in Jerusalem

Luke's opening paragraph (with its equivalent in Acts) reflects one distinctive concern of his Gospel, to put Jesus within the context of history. The dates he periodically gives fulfill the same function (e.g., Lk 1:5; 2:1-2; 3:1). This is a story that really happened on the stage of world history, and it has implications for world history from now on. The opening paragraph refers to a Gentile reader, Theophilus, who is perhaps interested in Jesus but has not yet quite committed himself. Nevertheless, Luke, like Matthew, writes from the perspective of the church.

One of his ways of reflecting this perspective is his periodic references to the Holy Spirit, the one who brought the presence and power of God and of Jesus to believers who lived after Jesus' death and resurrection. Another is his interest in prayer: he refers often to Jesus' prayer life and tells more than the other Gospels of his teaching on the subject.

In this work that is to be continued in the story of the spread of the gospel through the world, in Acts, it was fitting for Luke to emphasize Jesus' concern for the outcast. That theme comes out in parables such as the Pharisee and the tax collector (Lk 18:9-14), and in stories such as that of Zacchaeus (Lk 19:1-9). Similarly he emphasizes Jesus' concern for the lost (in the parables in Luke 15 about the lost sheep, the lost coin, and the lost son) and the Samaritans (in the story of the good Samaritan in Luke 10). Luke alone tells of the mission of the seventy-two disciples (Lk 10:1-18), whose number suggests a reference to the nations of the world.

What most distinguishes Luke is the fact that it is only part one of a two-part work. The Acts of the Apostles is his part two, as its opening verses show. Luke, like the other believers, knew that Jesus' coming meant that "the last days" had dawned (Acts 2:17). But this dawning did not mean that the story of God's achieving his purpose was over. It continued in the story of the spreading of the gospel message through the world. Jesus had declared that his followers were to bear witness to him through the whole world—in Jerusalem, in all Judaea and Samaria, and to the ends of the earth (Acts 1:8). Acts shows how the gospel began to triumph in Jerusalem (Acts 1–7) and spread through Judaea and Samaria (Acts 8–12), both especially through the ministry of Peter. This latter section tells of how Saul/Paul came to believe in Jesus and of the first Gentile believers; from now on, attention is transferred from Peter to Paul, who carries the torch around the eastern Mediterranean and eventually as far as Rome itself. The program set by Jesus is thus implemented with the power, inspiration, and guidance of the Spirit.

God's own involvement is indicated by the ironies that Saul, the chief persecutor, becomes Paul, the most energetic missionary; and Jews and Romans unwittingly combine to make it possible for him to preach the gospel at the capital of the empire. The story is not so much of the Acts of the Apostles as of the Acts of the Holy Spirit, or rather of some of the Acts of the Holy Spirit, for the story of the first years of the church was a much broader one than is covered by Acts. The account of how the church spread from Jerusalem to Rome is fundamental to the history of the church from then on.

John

The fourth Gospel is a different world again. Gone is the rapid succession of quickly sketched scenes around Galilee, the successions of parables and miracle stories. John offers us a score of more carefully written, worked-out units, mostly against the background of Jerusalem. Perhaps his picture corresponds to what he had seen and heard there himself; perhaps it is a version elaborated as a result of his meditation and preaching over the years. A simple scene becomes the occasion or jumping-off point, often by means of conversation between Jesus and his hearers, for a long discussion of the issues involved in his ministry. They are simple scenes but often "mighty works." The stories are vivid: we can easily imagine the panic at Cana when the drink runs out (Jn 2), or the discreet visit of the uncomprehending Nicodemus who cannot quite make Jesus out (Jn 3), or Jesus' uninhibited conversation with a much-married foreigner at Jacob's well (Jn 4). A thread of gentle humor runs through the stories, often at the expense of the luckless Pharisees, unable to explain how Jesus could have healed a blind man and derided by the ordinary folk who are his parents for their inability (Jn 9), but also at the expense of almost equally uncomprehending disciples such as the gloomy Thomas: "Let's go to Jerusalem and die with him" (Jn 11:16).

Humor, pathos, and tragedy go together. Peter, challenged by Jesus as to whether the disciples will stick by him, opens his heart full of deep doubt and deep commitment: "Lord, to whom would we go? You have the words of eternal life" (Jn 6:68). The incomprehension of the Jewish leaders is amusing but also culpable and in a sense demonic. The polemic against "religiousness" without personal response to Jesus is stronger here than anywhere else in the Bible.

As the stories are memorable, so are the sayings. In particular, there recur Jesus' "I am" statements—the bread of life (Jn 6:35), the light of the world (Jn 8:12), the gate for the sheep (Jn 10:7), the good shepherd (Jn 10:11), the resurrection and the life (Jn 11:25), the way, the truth, and the life (Jn 14:6), the real vine (Jn 15:1). Each constitutes a claim to recognition as the only one who can really meet human needs, and an invitation to respond to him and prove him as such. The "I ams" are one of the marks of the more exalted picture of Jesus the Son of God that characterizes this Gospel.

At the beginning John speaks of Jesus as "the Word"—God's way of expressing himself—and the stories show him as God's revelation or God's message. At the end, Thomas acknowledges him as "my Lord and my God" (Jn 20:28). In John, Jesus speaks more openly and systematically about his relationship with his Father. He also speaks more of the personal relationship between himself and his Father on the one hand and that of those who believe in him on the other, a relationship to be developed by the coming of the Holy Spirit to the disciples after Jesus' departure. But the Jesus of John's Gospel is also pictured in his humanity as clearly as anywhere in the Bible: tired, thirsty, weeping, troubled, questioning. John's statement of his purpose in writing indicates that he aimed to lead his readers to the belief that this Jesus (the figure of history) is the Christ, the Son of God (Jn 20:31).

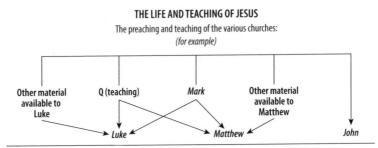

THE LIFE AND TEACHING OF JESUS

The preaching and teaching of the various churches:
(for example)

Other material available to Luke

Q (teaching)

Mark

Other material available to Matthew

Luke   *Matthew*   *John*

Figure 7.1. How the Gospels may have come into existence

PART III

THE WORD OF GOD TO HIS PEOPLE

W E HAVE BEEN SURVEYING HOW God is one who has been doing things in world history as a whole, in Israel's story, in Jesus' coming, and in the life of individuals.

God is also one who has been speaking. From Jeremiah's day comes a threefold categorization of the people through whom one might expect to learn: priests, experts, and prophets (Jer 18:18). Subsequent to Jeremiah's day there developed two further means by which a message came. In the New Testament, the apostles in their letters directed the people of God, in a way that was in some respects analogous to the earlier role of the prophets. And toward the end of each Testament there appears a book (Daniel and Revelation) that is more visionary and that gives a revelation concerning the end, when God's purpose will finally be brought to fulfillment.

8

THE INSTRUCTION OF THE PRIESTS

Exodus to Deuteronomy

EXODUS

Instruction is the business of priests. People would go to a priest for a ruling on some aspect of behavior. The priest was the expert in God's Torah, who could pronounce authoritatively concerning questions one might want to ask. Thus when Jesus had cleansed a man of his skin ailment, he sent him to the priests (Lk 17:14) to fulfill the procedures required of someone who was to be regarded as restored to the normal life of the community. The Torah was entrusted to the Levitical priests for the purpose of teaching the people (Deut 31:9; 33:10).

On other occasions, the Torah would contain no regulation that covered the inquiry made of it. If a priest was asked a question about a difficult problem or a special case, then he (and his colleagues, no doubt) would seek to establish what ruling was in accord with the mind of God and with the truth of God as they already knew it.

In some passages in the Torah, one may be able to see how the priests worked out the implications of some principle in this way. Thus Exodus 21:28-32 lays down the principle that a man is not to be held guilty of a capital offense if his ox kills someone. But what if the animal has killed before? Then he is guilty. What if the animal gores a child? The same rules apply. What if it gores someone's servant? Compensation is to be paid to the servant's master. (Many translations refer to "slaves" rather than "servants," but this is generally misleading; the reference is to temporary bondservants, not to people who were owned by their masters.) We may guess that the Torah as we have it in the Old Testament partly accumulated through the growth of case law in this way.

Sometimes the Torah simply lays down the bare general principle. Many of the Ten Commandments take this form: they simply look Israel in the eye and declare "There is to be no stealing" and so on. No special cases are specified; it's assumed that the meaning is clear. No sanctions are declared; to say "If you do that I'll . . ." weakens the force of the commandment by implying the assumption that it will be disobeyed.

Although the Torah connects all these instructions with Moses, and we can see them being taught and developed through the priesthood, much of their ultimate origins lay further back. The Ten Commandments' prohibition of adultery, theft, and so on would not be novel in Moses' day. Many provisions in the Torah make sense against the background of clan life before Moses' time. Many provisions have parallels in the teaching of other ancient peoples. The best-known example is the Law Code of Hammurabi, five centuries older than the time of Moses. These would be the kind of expectations that characterized the civilization from which Israel's ancestors came, as well as the civilization of the Canaanites among whom the Israelites lived.

While the Torah includes many parallels with other peoples' teaching, the Israelite versions have distinctive tendencies. They are often more humanitarian; stealing is not a capital offense, as it could be in Britain even in the eighteenth century and in the United States in the nineteenth century, and there is no mutilation of criminals by cutting off hands or feet. On the other hand, sometimes Israel's laws are stricter: adultery and many other offenses, as well as murder, are capital offenses, though the fact that there are no accounts of the execution of people guilty of such offenses suggests this sanction was more theory than practice. Israel's rules are more egalitarian than some other peoples': there is not one law for the rich, another for the poor. Indeed, they emphasize that justice is due to the weak. They are interested in compensation as well as punishment: there is no penalty for hurting someone in a fight, but you do have to pay for their lost time and take care of them until they get well (Ex 21:19).

It's possible, then, to claim the superiority of the Torah at some points, but it will also seem less enlightened than some laws of our own day, even though more enlightened than those of a century ago. The lower position of women strikes us, now that women are assumed to have the same rights as men. The Torah starts from where the people of their culture were. They are not a revelation of unrealizable ideals but a collection of attempts to make life more humanitarian than it might otherwise be.

LEVITICUS

We have noted that the Torah is the business of priests. Their particular concern is the instruction about worship that is concentrated in Leviticus. In moving on from the teaching in Exodus, we move from what we might think of as a statute book to a prayer book. Yet Israel made no sharp distinction between criminal law, social custom, moral precept, and worship rubric. They aimed to bring the whole of life under God's lordship.

So religious questions appear throughout the Torah, but Leviticus especially focuses on the requirements of religion. It puts into writing the regulations regarding different types of sacrifice (Lev 1–7), which were of great importance in a situation where sacrifice was the way by which the relationship between God and humanity was expressed and restored. Five chapters (Lev 11–15) describe what causes uncleanness or taboo and how it can be dealt with. A basic aim of this rule of life that God gave Israel was to embody the fact that Israel was no ordinary nation but one that had a distinctive place in God's purpose. God later told Jesus' followers to set aside these rules in order to reach out in a different way to the Gentile world.

These chapters in Leviticus lie behind the kosher regulations that still distinguish the Jewish people. One of the most striking appears not in Leviticus but in Exodus (twice) and Deuteronomy, the requirement not to cook a young sheep or goat in its mother's milk (Ex 23:19; 34:26; Deut 14:21). Perhaps this unlikely sounding barbarism was practiced in Canaanite religion; its background is obscure. But the rule has had great influence, as the rabbis decided that it would be safer never to cook meat and milk in the same vessels or let it be consumed in the same meal.

The later instructions in Leviticus 17–26 are more mixed: some concern ritual questions, others are directly ethical. Running through them is a concern for Israel's holiness: "You are to be holy, because I, Yahweh your God, am holy" (Lev 19:2). This motivation is mentioned in connection with all sorts of rules. To be holy is to be set apart for God. Israel is indeed called to be distinctive, and thereby to witness to the distinctiveness of its God.

Leviticus includes one of the accounts of Israel's religious festivals here (Lev 23). The list begins with the sabbath, a weekly day of rest. The Ten Commandments (Ex 20; Deut 5) suggest two reasons for the observance of the sabbath: it is an imitation of God in his creative activity (because he worked for six days and then rested), and it is a reminder of the mercy shown by God to the Israelites in Egypt (for as serfs there, they had no opportunity to rest). Sabbath observance became a distinctive mark of Israelites in the exile.

The sabbath principle is later extended (Lev 25) to the giving of a sabbath, or fallow, year to agricultural land. Then one sabbath year in seven was to be a "year of restoration" when debts were canceled. Land that had been leased was to be returned to its original owner, and bondservants were to be freed. The land belongs to God and, under God, to the families to whom he had allocated it (in the time of Joshua), so it cannot be sold; and people are made in God's image, so they cannot be "possessed."

The list of actual festivals begins with Pesah, Passover, in March-April. The Israelites were told to make this feast the beginning of their year (Ex 12), because it marked the event that constituted their beginning as a nation (see chap. 4). It is characteristic of Israel's religious festivals that they have a background both in the life of farmer or shepherd and in the history of the redemption of God's people—rather as Christmas and Easter are Christian festivals with pagan elements. Passover involved killing a lamb and daubing its blood on the doorposts of the house. This practice perhaps had its background in the annual cycle of the life of a nomadic shepherd. But the exodus from Egypt happened at the time of this festival, and it became part of the event of the exodus (Ex 11–13), part of the story of God's salvation of his people. It was at the time of Passover that Jesus was killed; thus Easter and Passover come at the same time of year. The New Testament sees Jesus' death as like the death of the Passover lamb, which made redemption possible.

Passover is accompanied by the first of the agricultural festivals, Flat Bread, when the old year's leaven is thrown out in anticipation of new crops. In terms of the exodus story, eating unleavened bread recalls the haste of the Israelites' departure from Egypt, which left no time for using yeast and waiting for the bread to rise (Ex 12:39).

The importance of Israel's agricultural life is indicated by the fact that Israel celebrated several harvest festivals. These began with the commencement of the barley harvest. The first sheaf to be gathered was taken to the priest (Lev 23:10). In other areas of life, too, the principle was accepted that the firstfruits went to God. The farmer gave God the first animal each mother bore (Ex 13:12). Even the firstborn of a human mother was God's by right (Ex 13:2). Whereas other nations sometimes sacrificed firstborn children to the gods, and Israelites did so in times of religious and moral degradation (see, e.g., Jer 7:31), the story of Abraham and Isaac (Gen 22) records that, while the willingness to make this great sacrifice is valued, the child is to be replaced by an animal.

Seven weeks after the offering of the first sheaf, the completion of the barley harvest was celebrated, at Pentecost. Here Leviticus breaks out of its concern with worship to note that at harvest the edges of the fields are to be left so that poor people, and foreigners who have no land of their own to harvest, may help themselves.

Before the final harvest festival came two other occasions. The calendar year began (as it still does in Israel) in September-October, "the seventh month" if you reckon from Passover. This is the beginning of the agricultural year: the rains are due to come after the long drought of summer. Nature will be able to come to life again, and plowing for the next year's crop will be possible. The beginning of the year is celebrated by a special day of rest; lesser celebrations were included to mark the beginning of each month.

Ten days later comes the most solemn day of the year, Yom Kippur, Expiation Day, when an annual ritual is to be performed to take away the offenses of the people (Lev 23:26-28). The ritual for the day (Lev 16) involved first sacrificing a goat in the temple. Then the high priest laid hands on another goat, an act that symbolized the transfer to it of the people's sins, before it was driven off into the desert.

The Expiation Day was in turn followed by a final great occasion of joy, celebrating the full gathering in of the harvest. It was called Sukkot, "Shelters," and it recalled not only the practice of sleeping out of doors in makeshift bivouacs during the harvest but also the necessity of living in these simple shelters after the people left Egypt.

DEUTERONOMY

I have said something about Deuteronomy in chapter five. Here is the most systematic exposition of God's requirements of his people within the covenant. The book begins by making it clear that God is not interested in a mere outward response to what he has done for them. He wants to be their only God; he wants the love of heart, soul, and strength (Deut 6:4-5). Jesus took this as the foremost of the commandments (Mt 22:37); the second most important was the command from Leviticus 19:18 that we should love our neighbor as a person like ourselves. To all Jews, these verses in Deuteronomy 6 are the center of their creed, the ones they recall most often.

Deuteronomy goes on to itemize the personal response God looks for from his people: trust in him, reverence for him, loyalty to him. They are continually to recall the blessings he has shown to them. They are to give concrete expression to their response in detailed obedience to his instructions. The content of these instructions is similar to that of the instructions in Exodus, Leviticus, and Numbers. A distinctive feature of Deuteronomy is the systematization of God's demands. Deuteronomy 12–26 cover the life of the people of God very broadly: worship, mourning practices, food, giving, the treatment of servants, festivals, the administration of justice, the conduct of war, the detection of crime, sexual purity, divorce, and remarriage. The whole of life, corporate and individual, is to be brought under the lordship of God, so that in every way Israel can embody what it means to be "God's own people."

The theology of Deuteronomy is beautifully balanced: grace and obedience, God's act and people's response, inner attitude and outward practice, the call to obedience and the warning of punishment—these are finely set in relation to one another. But the instructions demand what will not be given. The heyday of Deuteronomy was the reform of Josiah (see chap. 2). But this reform was a failure. There was nothing wrong with the Torah, but there was something wrong with the people to whom it was given. It needs to be written on their minds, not merely on stone tablets, before they will obey it (Jer 31:33). Or, as Deuteronomy puts it, God will have to *give* them obedient minds so that they will love him (Deut 30:6).

It is not that the expectations of the Torah are so demanding or onerous, and we have noted that the Jewish people do not see the Torah as a burden. It is the gracious gift of God, and fulfilling it is a way of responding to him. The Torah is thus a source of joy for a Jew. One of the most joyous occasions of the year is the feast of "Rejoicing in the Torah." While the festival does not go back to the Old Testament, this rejoicing features there in the lyrical enthusiasm shown by some of the Psalms (especially Ps 119, with its 176 verses of enthusiasm over the Torah).

The New Testament notes that it is possible to have an entirely different perspective on the Torah. There were believers in Jesus who wanted to impose obedience to the Torah on Gentile believers in Jesus as well as on Jewish believers in Jesus. That imposition compromises the basis on which God relates to Gentiles, and on which God now relates to Jews. There is still much to learn from the Torah, but its status within the covenant has changed.

9

THE MESSAGE
OF THE PROPHETS

Isaiah to Malachi

Fifteen books in the Bible, between Isaiah and Malachi, are named after prophets. In English Bibles, Lamentations and Daniel also come in this section of the Bible; but they appear elsewhere in the Hebrew Bible, and I am leaving them to chapters thirteen and fourteen.

In the Hebrew Bible the story from Joshua to Kings is regarded as part of the Prophets, and this outlook reflects an important feature about prophecy: it is tied up with historical events. The prophets brought a message from God that reflected God's involvement in and lordship over the history of their day.

The heyday of prophecy is the time when Israel had kings—the time from Saul to the exile, and then the time during and just after the exile, when there was some hope of a reestablishment of the monarchy. The kings were always in danger of ruling in a way that ignored the fact that God was the real King of Israel. The prophets could speak a word from God that confronted the institutional leadership of the state. They could be the means of

God's will being declared when the kings were opposed to God's will. We can see figures such as Samuel, Nathan, Ahijah, Elijah, Elisha, Amos, Isaiah, and Jeremiah acting in this way.

Something novel occurs with the appearance of Amos, Hosea, Isaiah, and Micah, in the eighth century before Christ; for the first time prophets have books named after them that collect their teaching, as well as sometimes relating incidents from their lives. These prophets are no longer merely figures in the story related in Samuel and Kings: indeed, only Isaiah and Jonah are mentioned there (Haggai and Zechariah appear in Ezra). The eighth century is the beginning of the time when Israel is under the influence or control of the great empires (Assyria, Babylon, Persia, and later Greece) and when God is threatening to use these empires to bring judgment on Israel—or later, to bring restoration.

Not everything in each book was uttered by the prophet whose name appears at the head of the first chapter. It is not that the books are anthologies, but the original sayings of a prophet have been expanded by his followers, whom God also used to bring new messages to a later day in the spirit of the prophet to whom they looked back, or to repreach their messages in a new situation. The clearest example is the book of Isaiah. Isaiah bade his disciples to "guard and preserve the messages" that God gave him (Is 8:16) until the time they were fulfilled. The exile, a century and a half later, formed the vindication of the darker side of these messages, and now there arose new prophets "in the spirit of Isaiah" who declared that his message was fulfilled and preached the new message that Isaiah would now bring. Consequently, their preaching appears within the book of Isaiah, rather than forming a separate book. Some of the other books (especially Jeremiah, Ezekiel, Micah, and Zechariah) have also been expanded to a greater or lesser extent. We have here, then, not merely the message of one prophet in one century, but the additional messages of further prophets or preachers who bring the word of God to a later age.

Why did these prophets, beginning in the eighth century, come to have books named after them? With Amos a new feature came into Israel's religion. Until his day, the events that fundamentally decided Israel's faith had been things God did in the past—the events from Abraham through the exodus from Egypt and the entry into Canaan to the establishment of the monarchy, the capture of Jerusalem, and the building of the temple. Amos declares that the event of which Israel has most to take into account is still to come: it is the day of Yahweh, the day of the Lord. Furthermore, there is a radicalism about the message of these prophets, which goes beyond merely turning Israel around to face the future instead of the past. They also declare that the future will be unpleasant. This day of Yahweh will be darkness, not light (Amos 5:18-20). It means, in fact, the end of life as Israel knows it, unless Israel turns from its moral waywardness, the selfishness of its community life, its religious unfaithfulness, and its political pragmatism.

The prophets were thus both foretellers and forth-tellers. They declared events that were to take place: when Israel was characterized by waywardness and self-confidence they declared judgment, when its faith and morale had gone (in the exile) they brought a message of future restoration. In this sense they were foretellers. They were not people who could merely read the signs of the times. Often their message went against what was politically likely; it was based on what God told them, a revelation related to what was morally and theologically demanded, even if it was not politically inevitable. As well as speaking of the future, however, they proclaimed or told forth God's demands of the present moment. A key word that recurs is *repentance* or "turning." The people have *turned* away from God, and they risk him *turning* away from them unless they *turn* back. Repentance is not a mere feeling of sorrow but a re-direction of the whole person. God's demand is that, in the light of what the prophet says about the future, they should turn around their lives in the present.

In speaking thus, they saw themselves as God's messengers or aides. An earthly king had messengers to make his pronouncements. The messengers would say, "The king says, inasmuch as such-and-such is the case, I declare that such-and-such will happen." Similarly the prophet declares, "God says, inasmuch as such-and-such is the case [his people have rebelled against him], I declare that such-and-such will happen [they will go into exile]." As God's representatives, prophets use many means to get their point home: they can declare a curse on the people (like a human being cursing another human being), they can lament the people's unfaithfulness (like someone sorrowing over the unfaithfulness of their spouse), they can sing a dirge over the doomed nation (like the mourners at a funeral), they can tell parables and riddles to get attention and then capitalize on it. In every way they seek to drive home the crucial message they have been given.

It is worth trying to appreciate the outward form of these different types of message. All the individual examples of a particular type have their distinctive points: but there is something to learn from the outward shape that they may have in common. This point may be appreciated if we consider how we ourselves learn a lot simply from the outward form and shape of things that we read or hear or see. This was so when letters were a key means of communication. People might receive several different types of letter: one typed on headed notepaper from a business concern, another handwritten, another printed. The language they used might differ: formal and legal, or personal and friendly, or in the enthusiastic superlatives of an advertising circular. Before people read the specific message, they knew "how" to read it: what allowances to make for exaggeration, what to read between the lines. Then they would find that (for instance) an advertising circular could be written in the form of a personal letter or of a consumer report, so that it achieved (or it hoped to achieve) a different kind of impact. Similarly, the prophets achieved different kinds of impact by taking up the varied speech forms of everyday life and utilizing them for their religious purpose.

There was power in a prophet's words, as there was power in the words of a king's messenger. They were bound to come true if the prophet was sent by God. Further, prophets did more than preach the message—they acted it out. When Jeremiah broke a clay jar (Jer 19), it was not merely a piece of drama. Because Jeremiah was commissioned by God, his actions, too, put God's will into effect. Breaking the jar set the wheels in motion for the breaking up of the state. Thus efforts were often made to shut the prophets up (see Jer 20). They were dangerous people.

ISAIAH

The book of Isaiah falls into clear divisions.

1–12. Isaiah indicts the people of Judah in the time of King Ahaz (about the 730s before Christ). Judah is enthusiastic about its worship but full of moral rebellion and unfaithfulness between people, and in practice it does not trust its God but tries to protect itself by deft political alliances. Isaiah warns of God's judgment but promises that God will eventually restore Israel: the section ends with a psalm of praise for Israel to sing "on that day."

13–23. Isaiah declares that God's judgment will also fall on other nations: Babylon, Moab, Damascus, Ethiopia, Egypt, Assyria, Dumah, Arabia, Tyre. While his indignation reflects the nations' opposition to Judah, the prophecies are addressed to Judah itself. To Judah they form another warning not to rely on these peoples and also an encouragement not to be afraid of them. In addition, on one hand, Isaiah includes Jerusalem in the condemnations to make it clear that it is in no better a position than anyone else, and on the other hand, he promises mercy and blessing for many of these other nations, as well as speaking of their judgment.

24–27. This section includes further pictures of judgment and restoration, but the references are less political and less specific. The picture is more one of universal judgment and of resuscitation.

28–35. This section includes more indictments of Judah, warning of judgment but promising that God will eventually restore Judah, when "the desert will rejoice and flowers will bloom in the wilderness." The chapters parallel Isaiah 1–12, but these messages belong to a later period, especially to the reign of King Hezekiah (about the 700s before Christ), and the challenge to trust in God becomes the central feature.

36–39. These chapters reflect the same period, the reign of Hezekiah; these are not messages *of* Isaiah, however, but stories *about* Isaiah similar to those recorded in 2 Kings. They look forward, beyond the reign of Hezekiah, to the exile of Judahites to Babylon, which will happen more than a century later.

40–55. This section presupposes the situation nearly two centuries later when Jerusalem has not only been destroyed (which happened in 587 BC) but many Judahites have been in exile in Babylon for fifty years. In light of that fact, the chapters introduce a new note: here "comfort" to the distressed is the center of the message. God is about to defeat Babylon and free people to go back to Judah (as happened in 539 BC).

56–66. These chapters are again less specific in reference. They are like Isaiah 1–12 in that they challenge the people about their waywardness and disobedience, but they reflect the situation in Judah after the fall of Babylon in 539, when the return promised in Isaiah 40–55 has been achieved but all is still not as it should be. The whole book closes with a promise of a new Jerusalem.

The book of Isaiah thus speaks to many different periods and takes up many different themes, but a feature that runs through it is the frequency with which the whole book describes Israel's God, Yahweh, as "the Holy One of Israel." That title for God comes only thirty times in the Bible, and twenty-five of them are in Isaiah, spread through the book. Isaiah is the book of the Holy One of Israel. The title comes in some psalms (Ps 71:22; 78:41; 89:18; also Jer 50:29; 51:5), and perhaps has its origin in the worship of the temple, but the book of Isaiah made it its own. There is a link with the vision that gave Isaiah himself his commission: "Holy, holy, holy is Yahweh Almighty," the seraphs proclaimed. That vision of the Holy One lies behind the book as a whole (see fig. 10.1).

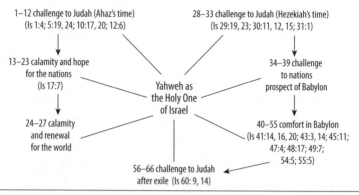

Figure 10.1. The book called Isaiah as the book of the Holy One of Israel

Isaiah is a man of Jerusalem, of the temple, and of the royal court. He knows that God committed himself to Jerusalem, that he chose Jerusalem as his city, that the temple in Jerusalem is his home, that the king who rules in Jerusalem is God's representative. He also knows that God is a God of justice and a "jealous" God who does not look lightly on people who are unfaithful to him. This places Isaiah in a dilemma. The social and moral life of Jerusalem is rotten; therefore Jerusalem deserves judgment. The leaders of Judah fail to trust in God and instead implement the pragmatic policy of shrewd political deals with various nations around; therefore they deserve judgment. But this is God's city, and the king is God's anointed.

Isaiah therefore declares that Jerusalem must be disciplined, but it will not actually fall. At the crucial moment God will rescue his people from the invader and punish him. The kings must be chastised, but the line of David will not be cast off. Some of the passages that are used in church at Christmas time (Is 9:2-7; 11:1-5) express this promise of a king who will really live up to the Davidic ideal.

Another motif by means of which Isaiah reconciles God's faithfulness to Israel with the necessity of punishing Israel is the idea of a remnant or remains. He calls his son Shear-Jashub, "A remainder will come back" (Is 7:3). The phrase could suggest several ideas, in all of which Isaiah may have seen some truth. One is that only some remains will escape the calamity God is bringing and return to the Promised Land. The name is thus a message of judgment. At the same lime it could suggest a message of hope—"at least some remains will come back." In this sense, all will not be lost. The phrase can then refer to coming back in repentance to God (not merely physically returning to the land): it contains an implicit moral challenge as to whether the hearer belongs to "the remains," the few who turn to God. Understood with various emphases, this idea of "the remainder" was of lasting theological importance.

Isaiah's conviction that Judah must undergo a terrible disciplining links with his experience of seeing God (Is 6). There in the temple, perhaps in the course of one of the great services when the congregation as a whole rejoiced in God's presence, Isaiah had a vision of God himself, with seraphs proclaiming "holy, holy, holy," and God appealing for someone to declare the message of judgment to his people. Because Israel's God is the Holy One, Israel must be disciplined, even though it is his people.

Later in Isaiah 40–55 the fact that God is the Holy One of Israel is no longer a threat but an encouragement. When Israel is in exile, having undergone the punishment that the earlier chapters declared (and more), the prophecy promises that the demoralized exiles can have their faith built up, because "the Holy One of Israel" is their restorer.

So who is the prophet who speaks in Isaiah 40–55? At first sight, since the chapters belong to the same book as the earlier prophecies of Isaiah, it seems that these too must be Isaiah's words. But the speaker speaks as one living in the exile. This prophet does not merely predict exile and restoration, as Isaiah could have done. He speaks of the exile as being almost over. The implication is that these are the words of someone who lived at this later period. The final chapters of the book (Is 56–66) then come from a further prophet or prophets who ministered back in Canaan later still. All these prophets looked at matters from a similar perspective to that of Isaiah himself (and thus their work was included in the collection that bears his name). They were all prophets of "the Holy One of Israel."

The author of Isaiah 40–55 can be thought of as a "Second Isaiah." Although he had many points in common with the "First Isaiah," he has his own distinctive characteristics. One difference, that his message is one of hope, not fundamentally of judgment, derives from his historical situation. Second Isaiah also emphasizes the exodus—in the sense that the return from exile will be a new exodus even better than the first—whereas first Isaiah had not mentioned the exodus. Whereas First Isaiah had emphasized the Davidic king, Second Isaiah does not speak of a Davidic Messiah. He sees the whole people as now given the special relationship with God that once belonged to David (Is 55). The people are called to be God's servant—though the prophet realizes that they cannot live up to this calling. Second Isaiah depicts what the calling of God's servant involves. It demands the acceptance of suffering and affliction, but God promises that such acceptance can bear fruit, because it will be the means of reconciling God and humanity.

Jeremiah

The book of Jeremiah cannot be divided into clear sections like the book of Isaiah—though Jeremiah 1–25 is mostly concerned with the teaching of Jeremiah, Jeremiah 26–45 with stories about Jeremiah, Jeremiah 46–51 with his indictments of other nations (these are similar to Isaiah 13–23), and Jeremiah 52 is a tailpiece that repeats the story at the end of 2 Kings relating how Jerusalem was taken and Jeremiah's prophecies were thereby proved true.

Jeremiah 1–25: Jeremiah's message

1	His call
2–6	Judah's apostasy and waywardness, and its punishment
7–10	Further warnings about false trust in the temple, in the word and in images
11–20	The rejection of God's message and the persecution of the messenger
21–24	Further warnings from the time of Zedekiah
25	His review of his twenty-three years of ministry from his call to 604

Jeremiah 26–45: Jeremiah's life

26–35	The demand of God's message (a)
26–29	Three parallel stories emphasizing that the more stubbornly people resisted Jeremiah's message, the worse their trouble
30–33	But the darkest hour is the dawn of hope: God does not intend judgment to be the end
34–35	The choice: be like the nation, which continues to rebel and must be judged (34), or be like the few who keep their commitments (35)

Jeremiah 46–51: Jeremiah's messages about other nations

Jeremiah 52: Epilogue—how the message came true

The presence of so many stories about Jeremiah is a striking feature of the book. There are few comparable stories in the books of the other prophets. Jeremiah begins by telling us how he came to be called to be a prophet; the story of his call provides the justification for the ministry he goes on to exercise. He tells us about many events in his ministry, for instance about some of the occasions on which he received a message from God (e.g., on a visit to a pottery [Jer 18]) and on which he delivered a message of God (e.g., in the temple [Jer 25]). Many of the stories relate what reaction Jeremiah's message received, and here lies their significance. Jeremiah may have been no more unsuccessful than other prophets (prophets were usually failures), but the personal opposition he received is sharper than that recorded of prophets such as Isaiah. The stories about him are stories of how he is thrown in the stocks, threatened with death, imprisoned in an empty water cistern, and mocked by other prophets. Jeremiah brings God's message, and what people think of God's message is expressed in what they do to the messenger.

Outside the stories about Jeremiah, the same point lies behind those sections of Jeremiah's poems in which he pours out his heart to God with a frankness and urgency unparalleled in the Bible outside the Psalms (Jer 11–20). These protests of Jeremiah tell us the inward story of his sufferings, of the cost that being a prophet brought to him personally. In the case of Jeremiah, God's message and God's messenger become hard to distinguish. Jeremiah is identified with God; so how people treat Jeremiah expresses what they think of God.

There are parallels between Jeremiah's message and that of Isaiah a century previously. Both declared that judgment must come on the people of God. There are also differences, which arise in part out of their background. Isaiah had been a man at home in Jerusalem, and he was used to thinking of it as God's dwelling place. Thus he had seen clearly that God was committed to Jerusalem and to the Davidic kings, and had promised that God would rescue Jerusalem and be faithful to his promise to David. Isaiah had been proved right; Jerusalem had escaped by a miracle from the attacks of King Sennacherib. You could say that Isaiah's message was vindicated too well. People came to trust too confidently in the eternal security of Jerusalem. When Jerusalem came under pressure again in Jeremiah's day, there were prophets prepared to reiterate Isaiah's message and say that Jerusalem would be safe because God would look after it. Their preaching could be backed up by the fact that Judah had reformed itself in the reign of King Josiah. Therefore God was bound to be on its side.

Thus Jeremiah had to dissent from some strong and plausible theological lines. The reform of Josiah was not enough, he declared (though he supported it when Josiah initiated it): the evils of human hearts had not been changed by the external measures that Josiah had imposed. The message of Isaiah, applicable though it may have been in Isaiah's day, was inappropriate now.

Jeremiah was the prophet to deliver this message because he was a very different person from Isaiah. He was not a Jerusalemite. He came from a village called Anatot, which was only three miles north of Jerusalem but lay across the crucial boundary between the areas of Judah and Benjamin. He belonged, therefore, to the north rather than to the south. His kinsfolk would not be oriented to Jerusalem to the same extent as Judahites were. This was still more the case if we are right to assume that the priestly family to which he belonged (Jer 1:1) was the one that had been excluded from the Jerusalem priesthood in the time of Solomon (1 Kings 2).

Being naturally less interested in Jerusalem than Judah was, the northern clans were apparently more attentive to the earlier theology of the exodus and the covenant. The exodus is not mentioned in prophets such as Isaiah and Micah—God's choice of Jerusalem and David is everything. It is the northern prophets who speak of the exodus faith. Although Jeremiah preached in Jerusalem, he was a northern prophet. Thus he calls Jerusalem back to the faith lying behind God's choice of Jerusalem and David, to the earlier story of God's making of his covenant with Israel in the time of Moses. It was a story that emphasized the moral, social, and political implications of a relationship with

God (Isaiah, of course, had been aware of these) and declared that judgment, and specifically exile, would come upon those who did not take the exodus faith seriously.

It was perhaps inevitable that Judah should prefer the comfortable message of its own prophets, based on the earlier messages of their great predecessor Isaiah, to the strange indictments of this nervous young man from across the border.

Not that Jeremiah's picture is all gloom. He, too, includes prophecies about the nations that are in some ways an encouragement to Judah. He also explicitly promises that the other side of judgment there is hope (Jer 30–33). The covenant is finished, but God will make a new one when people's deep religious and moral problem will be solved by the writing of the Torah into their minds, the reforming of their characters from the inside. The exodus is to be undone by an exile, but then there will be a new exodus to outshine the first and make the first exodus not worth speaking of. The Davidic monarchy is doomed, but then it will be reestablished, with kings to live up to their names. Zedekiah means "Yahweh is my faithfulness," but he ignored God's claims. Jeremiah promises that there is going to be a king who will live up to the name "Yahweh is our faithfulness."

Jeremiah put his money where his mouth was. At the height of the siege of Jerusalem, he agreed to buy a plot of land in Anatot. Humanly speaking, it was a laughable gesture: what use is owning land when an enemy is taking over the whole country? But Jeremiah knew that the God who was bringing judgment would bring restoration; the time for cultivating land would come again. A prophet always confronts his people's attitudes. When they are confident, he issues warnings. When the moment of despair comes, it is the time for a message of hope.

EZEKIEL

Ezekiel's ministry coincided with the later part of Jeremiah's— the years just before and just after the fall of Jerusalem in 587. But he prophesied in Babylon, not in Jerusalem, so we never see the two of them together. Ezekiel was among the first groups of Judahites to be taken into exile after Nebuchadnezzar's first siege of Jerusalem in 597. His calling then in Babylon was to prepare his fellow Judahites for the worse calamity that was still to come.

Like the people left in Judah, the Judahites taken into exile in 597 could not believe that the city would ever be destroyed. They assumed that their exile would be short and that they would soon be back home. Ezekiel's task was to keep repeating that the Judahites' unfaithfulness to God made it inevitable that a worse judgment should come.

1–3	Call: to speak of judgment
4–24	Judgment on Israel
25–32	Judgment on the nations
33	Call: to speak of restoration
34–48	Restoration for Israel

The first half of the book of Ezekiel reiterates this message that Ezekiel preached between 597 and 587. In the arrangement of the book, the transition to a more encouraging message begins with Ezekiel 25–32, where Ezekiel declares that God's judgment will fall on the other nations, too. They are especially condemned for their personal hostility and vindictiveness toward Israel. The explicit good news for Israel begins in Ezekiel 33. News arrives from Jerusalem that the city has finally fallen and the temple has been destroyed. At the moment of disaster Ezekiel's message changes. Now that the warning of judgment has been fulfilled, the way to restoration and blessing is open. God will give Israel leaders who lead it in the right way, he will recreate it from within, bring back to life the corpse it has become, win a final great victory over evil, rebuild the temple, and come to dwell among the people again (Ezek 33–48).

The way Ezekiel describes both Judah's sin and the nature of God's restoration of Judah reflects his background. Like Jeremiah he came from a priestly family, but unlike Jeremiah he belonged to the official priesthood of Jerusalem. His cast of mind is that of a priest. When he pictures the sin of Jerusalem, it is the sin of Israel's religious life, the temple defiled by idolatrous worship. When he pictures God's judgment, it is in terms of God's glory leaving the temple. When he pictures restoration, it is in terms of the building of a new and glorious temple.

Ezekiel is no ordinary priest. He is a man of extraordinary personality. With Ezekiel everything is larger than life, three-dimensional, quadraphonic, full frontal, IMAX. At nearly every point, he is like the other prophets, only more so. He begins by telling of his call: but the story of his call is twice as long as anyone else's, an extraordinary vision of the throne of God and a voice from heaven summoning him to eat a scroll full of declarations of judgment. He acts out in parabolic dramas the coming siege of Jerusalem (Ezek 4) and the departure of further refugees from the city. He is transported in a vision from Babylon back to the Jerusalem temple itself (Ezek 8), and he describes the enormities of the worship offered there. He relates complex allegorical indictments of the wanton whoring of Jerusalem, the bride of God (Ezek 16). Then the same range of gifts is used to paint the picture of a more glorious future: the valley of dry bones (just how Israel feels [Ezek 37]), the battle with Gog and

Magog (Ezek 38–39), the new temple with its stream of living water bringing life wherever it flows and allowing even the Dead Sea to abound in fish (Ezek 40–47), the repossessed land, and the city now called "Yahweh-Is-Here" (Ezek 48:35).

Have these pictures ever come true? The nation was reformed, the land repossessed, and the temple rebuilt when some of the exiles were allowed to return to Palestine by the Persians. But it was by no means as grand as the vision suggested by Ezekiel. The New Testament sees some of the promises given by Ezekiel as in a sense fulfilled through Jesus the Messiah. He is the one from whom living waters flow (Jn 7:38). It sees other aspects of the picture of the new temple as suggesting something of the nature of heaven and of the "new Jerusalem" (Rev 21–22). Some Christians have seen Ezekiel as predicting events of our own day, or events soon to come (such as battles between Russia and America), but Ezekiel emphasizes that his message relates to the people he is ministering to, and it is hard to see why God would be showing Ezekiel events to take place millennia after his time and their time.

THE TWELVE SHORTER PROPHETIC BOOKS

The Old Testament closes with twelve books often called the Minor Prophets. The title is unfortunate, because it suggests that they are not very important, whereas page for page they are at least as important as the longer books that precede them. The word *minor* in the original Latin title implies only that they are shorter. Possibly they were put together because they conveniently fitted on one scroll, while Isaiah, Jeremiah, and Ezekiel each had a scroll of their own. Hosea is the longest and comes first; thereafter they mostly come in chronological order (see table 10.1).

Table 10.1. Chronology of the Prophets

Eighth Century	Seventh Century	Exile	Restoration
Isaiah	Jeremiah	(Isaiah 40–55)	(Isaiah 56–66)
Amos	Nahum	Ezekiel	Haggai
Hosea	Habakkuk	Zechariah	
Jonah	Zephaniah	Obadiah	
Micah	Malachi		
			Joel

Amos was a shepherd from Judah. In Israel there were professional prophets, like our professional clergy, whose job was to give advice, preach, and so on. Amos tells us that he did not come from a traditional prophetic family but was compelled by God to take up the task of a prophet and to preach in Ephraim, the area of the northern clans. His prophetic voice has a new tone. He doesn't merely give advice when asked for it, or even just intervene to say that one king is to be replaced by another, as Elijah and Elisha had done. He declares that the whole nation is doomed. God has a special relationship with Israel, but this means it is especially guilty for ignoring him. There is a moral rigor about Amos that especially distinguishes him.

Hosea, too, prophesied in Ephraim, and the content of his message was similar: the state will be brought down by God. The distinctive flavor of Hosea's message is provided by his insight into the love of God, which is as fundamental to God's character as is his holiness. Hosea knew in his own person the tension between love for his wife and rejection of her because she was unfaithful. He saw the same tension in God. Like Amos, he knew that God's holiness meant Israel had to be punished. Amos and Hosea were proved right when the northern state was destroyed by the Assyrians (722). But both Amos and Hosea knew that love lay behind God's judgment and that therefore judgment could not be God's last word, and they end on a note of hope.

Micah was a native of Judah who prophesied in Judah—like Isaiah, who has overshadowed him. His message is similar to Isaiah's, though he is more thoroughgoing in his declaration of judgment ("Zion will be plowed like a field / Jerusalem will become a pile of ruins" [Mic 3:12]). The book of Micah has prophecies of judgment and restoration, following each other in two sets: Micah 1–3 and Micah 4–5, then Micah 6:1–7:6 and Micah 7:7-20.

Nahum is concerned with the downfall of the empire of the Assyrians, epitomized by their capital city, Nineveh. Nineveh is seen as Yahweh's opponent, as "the lying, murderous city" (Nahum 3:1), as an enchanting whore (Nahum 3:4), as a cruel destroyer (Nahum 3:19). He thus encourages little Judah not to be overwhelmed by the power of its oppressor.

Habakkuk belongs to the same decades when Babylon was replacing Assyria as the dominant power of the Middle East. Habakkuk is troubled by the injustice he sees all around him and asks what God is going to do about it. God's response is to declare that he plans to use the up-and-coming Babylonians as his agent in punishing the wicked. Habakkuk is horrified: after all, the Babylonians deserve judgment themselves. God promises that their time will come. The book closes with a psalm praying for God to act.

Zephaniah, too, declares the punishment of both Judah and the nations on "the day of Yahweh," "the day when God will act," "the great day of Yahweh." But he looks beyond "the day when Yahweh shows his fury" to a day when the nations will turn to God, and Judah will rejoice in God being back with it.

Haggai prophesied at a time after judgment had come and the exiled Judahites had begun to return to their homeland. But life back in the Promised Land was not what they had hoped for, and they had abandoned trying to rebuild the temple. Haggai challenges people to make the rebuilding their first priority; then they will know stupendous blessing, the fulfillment of the promise to reestablish David's house.

Zechariah, Haggai's contemporary, speaks to the same situation. He too challenges the Judahites to keep up their commitment to God but lays greater emphasis on God's commitment to them. This commitment is described in a series of visions: of patrols reporting that all is quiet in the Persian empire (but God is going to disturb this quiet in restoring Jerusalem), of four ox horns being crushed (thus will Judah's oppressors be shattered), of a man surveying Jerusalem with a view to rebuilding its walls (but the city will spread too fast to keep up with and will be protected by God himself anyway), of the high priest accused but acquitted in heaven (God is restoring the temple worship), of a lamp stand (symbolizing God's watching over the world), of an airborne scroll inscribed with a curse on perjury and robbery (which will be eliminated), of a woman carried off to Babylon (the removal of idolatry from Judah), and of four more patrol chariots sent out to implement Yahweh's will. The later chapters of Zechariah offer further pictures (puzzling in detail) of the restoration of Judah and the punishing of the nations.

Obadiah declares that the Edomites, who were related to the Israelites but were their enemies, will be punished for their pride and cruelty. Whereas the Edomites took over much Judahite land, the Judahites will themselves rule Edom on God's behalf.

Malachi reflects the same circumstances as Haggai and Zechariah (though he lived slightly later), discouragement at the hard conditions of the so-called restoration. Malachi calls on priests and people to honor God in their lives and worship, and warns them that "the great and terrible day of Yahweh" is coming—though for those who obey him, "my saving power will rise on you like the sun and bring healing like the sun's rays" (Mal 4:1-2). Before that day, however, Elijah must come: the New Testament sees John the baptizer as fulfilling Elijah's role, while Jews to this day leave a place for Elijah at their Passover meal.

Joel is dominated by the picture of a plague of locusts. Locusts can completely destroy a country's food, and thus such a plague could mean total disaster. This calamity, then, speaks of the day of judgment, and Joel calls for repentance in the light of it. But he promises that God "will restore what you lost in the years when swarms of locusts ate your crops" (Joel 2:25). A great day of judgment is still to come, but so is a great day of blessing, when God pours out his spirit on everyone (Joel 2:28).

10

THE LETTERS
OF THE APOSTLES

Romans to Jude

I N SOME RESPECTS THE EPISTLES are the most surprising part of the Bible. They are just letters (*epistle* is an old word for letters). They are not sermons, though they include much exposition of Scripture (that is, of the Old Testament) and instruction on Christian behavior, and no doubt they were read out in church. They were not written as theological manuals, though they include much of the most profound theology in the Bible. Nor were they written with readers throughout the church in mind. They were part of a living relationship between certain people in particular situations during the first years of the church's life.

So most of them begin like letters ("From Paul . . . to the churches of Galatia: Grace to you and peace") and end like letters ("Signed: Paul"). They pass on messages, ask for greetings to be passed on to others, and contain snippets of information and comment that someone who is not inside the situation doesn't quite know how to take. Why were they important enough to be included when the Christians collected their holy writings together?

The answer is that they were not just the means of friends keeping in contact or of someone getting a favor done by someone else. They expressed the thinking of some sharp minds on questions of religion and behavior as these arose in the life of the early church. Some, at least, were read out like sermons in the services of the churches to which they were written. Sometimes they begin with a long section on the Christian faith and then change the subject to questions of behavior. Other letters interweave these two concerns all through. The combination of teaching on belief and behavior is characteristic, as it was with the covenant in the Old Testament. Belief and behavior are assumed to be linked closely together.

Even when they are discussing theology, ethics, and church government, the letters remain rooted in particular situations. They are not theoretical manuals or systematic expositions of Christian truth but a series of responses to specific needs. This is most clear in a letter such as 1 Corinthians, where Paul refers explicitly to the questions the Corinthians have asked him and to the news about them that he has received. He gives them instruction on sexual morality because they have asked him certain questions; he describes how worship should work because he has heard how theirs does not.

The occasional nature of the theology of these letters appears in the way the points are expressed as well as in the subjects treated. This theology is not abstract and theoretical; it doesn't often talk in terms of "the nature of reality" or "the ground of being" or of "two natures in one substance." It characteristically expresses itself in picture language. This picture language is particularly important in the way the significance of Christ's dying for us is worked out. Being a Christian is like being declared innocent when you were guilty, like being made free instead of being a slave, like being admitted to the presence of a great king, like being accepted as you are by someone who had a right to a grudge against you. Great theological words such as *justification, redemption,* and *atonement* had their origin in the everyday life of nonbelievers and believers in the first-century world.

So the fundamental reason why these letters were important was their content. But a second, and related, reason was their authorship, for they embody the teaching of the apostles. Except for Hebrews, they bear the names of apostles or of other people (such as Jesus' brother Jude) who could speak from experience of Jesus himself. These letters have more authority in the church than the profoundest theology that was to come later because they pass on an understanding of the significance of Jesus for the church from people who lived close to him and to his time.

There are admittedly doubts about the authorship of a number of these letters. It has been suggested that, for instance, 2 Peter was not written by Peter but by a later person who wanted to give expression to what Peter would have said if he were here now. Such a theory may seem unlikely, but it is difficult to disprove. It is difficult to prove, too, and the content of these letters stands even if they were produced by someone other than the one named at the beginning. The example of Hebrews shows that the church wasn't trying to hold onto all the letters written by apostles and no others.

PAUL'S LIFE AND LETTERS

Here is one possible scheme of approximate dates.

35	Jesus' appearance to Paul (Acts 9)
46–47	Paul's first missionary journey (Acts 13–14), from Antioch to Cyprus and Turkey, and back
48–51	His second missionary journey (Acts 15–18), from Antioch through Turkey and Greece to Corinth (from here 1 and 2 Thessalonians were written) then back via Ephesus to Caesarea and Jerusalem
53–58	His third missionary journey (Acts 18–21), from Antioch through Turkey to Ephesus and Greece (Galatians, 1 and 2 Corinthians, Romans, 1 Timothy, and Titus were written on the way)
59–63	His imprisonment in Caesarea and Rome (Acts 24–28) (Ephesians, Philippians, Colossians, Philemon, and 2 Timothy were written from imprisonment)

Romans is Paul's longest letter and his most systematic. It provides an outline of his understanding of the gospel for the church in the capital of the empire, which he hoped to visit on his way to Spain as he fulfilled his calling of spreading his gospel through the Gentile world. He had not founded the Roman church (as he had founded many other churches to which he wrote), and he doesn't assume the same authority in relation to it as he does over others. Equally, he has not had reason to be kept in detailed touch with the situation there, and he has little reason to be upbraiding it.

His gospel is summed up in two sentences that follow his opening greeting: the gospel "is God's power to save all who believe, first the Jews and also the Gentiles. For the gospel reveals how God puts humanity right with himself" (Rom 1:16-17). This gospel is then elaborated in an exposure of humanity's willful commitment to wrongdoing, which even the Torah cannot undo (Rom 1:18–3:20). Only God can undo it. By sending Jesus to die for us he made it possible for us to be put right with God and to start a new life, freed from the domination by wrongdoing that otherwise characterizes us (Rom 3:21–8:39). Lest this should seem to compromise the position of the Jewish people, Paul expounds how God is still committed to them (Rom 9:1–11:36). Then he reminds his readers how believers are called to respond to God's love by committing themselves to God, a commitment Paul itemizes in various ways (Rom 12:1–15:13) before closing with further details of his personal plans and lengthy greetings.

First Corinthians is hardly any shorter than Romans, but it is quite different in atmosphere. Here was a church that Paul founded and one from which he has had correspondence and independent news. At point after point what he hears appalls him. Whether he looks at their theology, their personal lives, or their worship, he finds much cause for concern. It is all the more appalling since it is accompanied by what strikes Paul as a naively conceited estimate of their spiritual maturity. It is in the course of his dealing with these vagaries that Paul puts on paper some of the paragraphs that we would have been most sorry not to have: his account of the origin of the Lord's Supper (the Holy Communion or Eucharist), his "hymn to love," and his exposition of the fact of Jesus' resurrection and its importance (Rom 11; 13; 15).

Behind the problems raised by the Corinthian believers are recurring dangers in the early church, fundamentally false attitudes that twist the nature of the faith. One is a negative attitude to the body—the belief that the soul is all that really matters. If this is so, then it does not matter how believers behave outwardly—their soul is not affected. On the contrary, Paul knows, Jesus came in the flesh, and what people do with their bodies affects their whole person. The view Paul is confronting is one aspect of what came to be called Gnosticism (see later under Colossians).

Paul perceives fundamental questions underlying sometimes trivial outward questions, and his approach is not just to give simple authoritarian answers to the problems the Corinthians raise but to take his readers to the heart of the issues that the questions involve and to expound the fundamental Christian truths whose perspective needs to be applied to the situation: the message of the cross, the fact that God's Spirit lives in them, the calling to be concerned for my brother and sister rather than for my rights, the importance of love, the fact of the resurrection.

Second Corinthians is called by that title because it is the later of the two letters to Corinth that appear in the Bible, but references in these letters indicate that there were other letters that the churches did not preserve in this way; 2 Corinthians is at least the third or fourth letter that Paul wrote to Corinth. Here we can see he is dealing with the same difficult congregation as before, but in a different way. It is perhaps not surprising if they have reacted against the straight talking embodied in 1 Corinthians. The fact that Paul has not kept to his plans to come to see them gives them the opportunity to accuse him of being weak-willed and inconsistent, good at writing angry letters but scared of eyeball-to-eyeball confrontation, claiming apostolic authority but lacking apostolic credentials. This leads Paul to show a different side of himself. He describes how the real credential of an apostle is the mark of the cross, and this mark he bears. Although Paul has had his mystical experiences, the heart of his Christian experience is his bearing the cross of Christ: in this he finds not despair but hope, because there he finds the comfort of Christ, and there he proves that the time when he is weak is paradoxically when he is really strong.

In *Philippians*, the theme of the suffering involved in being a Christian recurs. Here Paul calmly weighs against each other the relative merits of staying alive or dying so as to be with Jesus. Philippians is a letter full of rejoicing.

The combination of suffering and joy reappears in *1 Peter*. (Fewer of the letters of James, Peter, Jude, and John were included in the New Testament, so they are known by their author, rather than by their audience: but many of them, like Paul's, were written to churches in particular areas.) Suffering and joy is also a dominant theme in Revelation (see chap. 13), and we are reminded by its recurrence that to be a minister, or just an ordinary believer, was often a dangerous affair. Christianity was a subversive movement. It was subversive of Judaism (because it suggested that the Torah was finished). It was subversive of the Roman Empire (because it refused to give the emperor the homage that belonged only to God). Thus Christians often had to pay for their beliefs.

Galatians introduces us to another of the underlying attitudes among some believers that Paul saw as undermining the nature of the gospel. Many believers of Jewish background maintained that when people came to believe in Jesus they had to begin keeping the Torah. If the Corinthians undervalued the importance of our outward human life, the Galatians overestimated it. Thus Paul has to say to the Galatians the opposite of what he said to the Corinthians. Their relationship with Christ does not hang on keeping the Torah—they have been freed from all that.

Thus Galatians is dominated, to an even greater extent than Romans, by the question of how people are put right with God, the question of justification. People everywhere seek to make a mark for themselves and to get people to accept and admire them by doing things. In practice, though, we never seem able to do enough to be sure of this status. Galatians and Romans declare that we can have the status anyway, because God is willing to accept us without our achieving anything at all.

Paul's defense of his apostolic position in Galatians leads to his giving his own account of some of the key incidents in his life. He speaks of his devotion as a Jew, his ruthless opposition to the church, and of Jesus appearing to him and turning his life upside down. He goes into detail regarding his relationship with the Christian mission based on Jerusalem—his original independence of them, their acceptance of him, and his willingness to stand up to them when they were wrong. The letter unveils some of the fierce confrontations that went on within the Christian movement from the beginning, especially over the key question of the place of Gentiles within a movement that was thoroughly Jewish in its origin and background.

Ephesians and *Colossians* overlap considerably in their themes and include some of the most developed insights of Paul's theology, on who Jesus is, on what he has achieved, and on what it means to be his people. In Colossians Paul confronts beliefs present in other religions of his day and shows how faith in Jesus is different from and superior to them. Some of Paul's comments suggest that the Colossian believers, too, were being urged to accept Jewish practices such as circumcision, kosher laws, and keeping the sabbath and festivals. There were beliefs other than mainstream Jewish ones involved. The worship of angels (Col 2:18), and the downgrading of Jesus (whose supreme importance Paul therefore emphasizes [Col 1:15-20]), suggests the belief in a varied hierarchy of supernatural figures between humanity and God. At about this time the religion called Gnosticism was developing. Gnosticism means "knowledge-ism" and suggests that we get to God in heaven by having the secret doctrines and "passwords" that enable us to elude the hostile supernatural beings between us and God. Gnostics understood Jesus within this framework: Paul believes it is fundamentally mistaken. Jesus is too big for it, and the gospel is not an esoteric secret but a divinely revealed public message.

The letters to the *Thessalonians* are distinctive for their dealing with questions to do with the end of history and the end of the individual's life. People are not to be so intent on Jesus' coming that they give up work! Nor are they to be so overcome by grief when someone dies that they look as if they have no special reason for hope. First Thessalonians seems to be the earliest of Paul's letters in the New Testament, notable for its clearly formulated picture of the events to take place when Jesus comes.

THE OTHER LETTERS

The expectation of Jesus' coming is a central concern also of later letters such as *2 Peter* and *Jude*. Both emphasize that this event will be a moment of judgment on false belief, and 2 Peter warns lest anyone becomes slack in their Christian profession because the coming of Jesus seems delayed.

Hebrews is more like a sermon than a letter (though it ends with one or two greetings). We do not know who wrote it. It challenges its readers to take their Christian calling more seriously and to see that the church is called to a life of steadfast pilgrimage. They are to persevere and not waver. The title "Hebrews" reflects the letter's Jewish concern. It emphasizes the superiority of Jesus over various features of the Jewish religion, such as the importance of Moses, the revelation on Mount Sinai, the wilderness sanctuary and its sacrifices. These were all right in their way and in their time, but at every point Jesus fulfills the same function as they did and goes far beyond what they could achieve. Hebrews argues its points by taking sections of the Old Testament that discuss the themes it wants to take up and preaching a Christian sermon on these texts.

James is another sermon-like letter, and another Jewish document, though in a different sense. There is little that is explicitly Christian in it; if we omit the references to Jesus in James 2:1 and James 3:1, it could be an ordinary Jewish sermon. Its concern is the opposite of Galatians. Whereas the Galatian believers were inclined to overemphasize Christian obedience, James's audience takes it too lightly. Paul in Galatians (and Romans) says, "You are right with God not because you live in obedience to him but just because of trusting in Christ" (and adds, "You only have to look at Abraham for an illustration of that point"). James has to say the opposite: "You are not right with God just because of trusting in Christ: you have to live in obedience to him" (and James, too, adds, "You only have to look at Abraham for an illustration of that point"). The two emphases are designed to confront two different mistakes. So James concentrates on getting his readers to live lives worthy of the faith they profess.

First and Second John have the same atmosphere as John's Gospel, with many references to "light" and "life" and "love." But whereas the Gospel was written so that people might believe and have life (Jn 20:31), the letters were written so that people might *know* that they have life (1 Jn 5:13)—in other words, so that they would be sure of their position as believers. John points his readers to ways they can test their lives in order to see whether they really belong to Jesus.

The letters to *Timothy*, *Titus* and *Philemon*, and *3 John* are more personal. Philemon is the only really private letter, appealing for clemency to a runaway slave. Yet even this letter is part of the ministry of Paul as an apostle concerned with the relationship between his spiritual brother Philemon and his spiritual son Onesimus. The other three are written to leaders of churches, about how to fulfill their ministry. They emphasize the importance of establishing a stable ministry in the church, of seeing that the church holds on firmly to the Scriptures (the Old Testament) and to the truth about Jesus, and of guarding against false beliefs.

11

THE ADVICE
OF THE EXPERTS

Proverbs and Song of Songs

NEARLY ALL THE BOOKS WE HAVE LOOKED at so far are distinctively Israelite. The story of God and his people is the story of Israel, even though at the beginning and end of the story the point is made that the God of Israel is also the God of the whole world. The Torah is the rule of life to be kept by Israel; it is not binding on Gentiles. The prophets, even if they speak of the nations around, speak to Israel.

The advice in Proverbs and the poems in the Song of Songs do not refer to the great events of Israel's history such as the exodus or the building of the temple; there is little distinctively Israelite about them. They are concerned with life as it is lived every day by ordinary people. The scholars or experts whose insight appears here made it their business to try to understand what life was about by looking at it. They then say to us, "This is how life works; if you want to be happy and successful, you will live in harmony with these facts of life."

PROVERBS

In Proverbs, most of the advice comes in the form of sayings just one verse long (the "proverbs" proper). They are collected in Proverbs 10–31, with little concern for arranging them by subject. Sometimes they are prosaic and down to earth in their advice, but often they offer striking figures of speech that bring a smile: "Beauty in a woman without good judgment is like a gold ring in a pig's snout" (Prov 11:22); "It is better to meet a mother bear robbed of her cubs than to meet a fool busy with a stupid project" (Prov 17:12); "The lazy man stays at home; he says a lion might get him if he goes outside" (Prov 22:13).

Yet the sayings are not interested only in the observation of life and in behavior that pays. They are concerned with right behavior, which they believe is the same thing as behavior that pays. Their moral exhortations are in fact parallel to the rules in the Torah: for example, "Don't move an old boundary mark that your ancestors established" (Prov 22:28; cf. Deut 27:17).

The parallels between the sayings of the experts and the rules of the priests suggest they have a common background. Both are at home in the teaching of the family, and we can imagine them as the topics of teaching given by parents in the clan life of Israel's ancestors. This teaching was then passed on in the nation of Israel by two routes, via the priests and via the experts.

The saying about boundary marks raises another issue. It is one of "Thirty Wise Sayings" that appear in overlapping form in an Egyptian work. Of all the Israelite writers, the experts were the most open to learning from other peoples. Obviously other peoples could not write the story of Israel, but they could write about their own observation of life, and from this Israelite teachers are willing to profit.

There is a third kind of learning and advice that appears in the sayings of the experts. As well as offering advice on what is sensible and on what is right, they talk about what is godly. Although they are trying to get as full a picture as possible of how life is and how it should be, they recognize that a total picture will inevitably elude them, for there remain enigmas about life. When we have done everything we can, we are still dependent on God: "You can get horses ready for battle, but it is Yahweh who gives victory" (Prov 21:31). "A nation without God's guidance is a nation without order. Happy is the man who keeps God's law" (Prov 29:18). Here the concern of the proverbs is close to that of the prophets, who sought to get Israel to take account of God's involvement in its life, to trust in him, and to pay attention to the demands of his will.

It would be misleading to suggest that Proverbs only brings in God when it reaches the mysteries at the edge of human experience. Although the book is concerned with secular life, it does not take a secular approach. On the contrary, its belief in God underlies all its teaching. It examines the world, but it believes the world is God's—it reflects his mind, resulting as it does from his creative activity.

This point is made explicit in Proverbs 8:22-31, where God's own insight speaks and describes its role as architect in God's creative work (or rather, so describes her role—insight is personified as a woman in Proverbs).

Like that paragraph, the other sections of the opening chapters of Proverbs (Prov 1–9) come in longer units than the one-verse couplets that characterize Proverbs 10–31. Those opening chapters also have a narrower range of interests. Two main themes recur. One is a repeated encouragement to take insight seriously—Proverbs 8 systematically expounds insights's invitation to pay attention. The other is a recurrent exhortation to avoid entanglement with other women. While this second theme is intelligible when understood in the straightforward sense, why should it be given such prominence? In the prophets, sexual unfaithfulness is often a way of describing Israel's failure of commitment to God, and here in Proverbs the warning against unfaithfulness implies an exhortation to stay committed to Yahweh, or to stay committed to expertise or good sense; the two major themes of Proverbs 1–9 are thus connected. Yahweh's teaching is good sense. Young men are urged not to let their attention wander elsewhere.

THE SONG OF SONGS

So the idea of faithfulness or unfaithfulness to God could be spoken of in terms of faithfulness or unfaithfulness to a human partner. In the Old Testament, Hosea makes this point in connection with his own marital experience, and in the New Testament Paul speaks of marriage as a picture of the relationship between Christ and his "bride," the church (Eph 5:21-33).

Many Jews and Christians have valued the love poems in the Song of Songs as a reminder of the loving relationship that exists between God and his people. In themselves, however, they are love poems, enthusing over the beauty of the loved one and over the experience of the loving relationship. They have been described as an extended commentary on Genesis 2:18-25. Those verses describe the origin of the complementary relationship between man and woman, and these poems explore that God-created bond in articulating the experiences and feelings of people on the way to their lifelong mutual relationship.

Song of Songs means "most beautiful of songs" (Song 1:1), as
Holy of holies means "Most holy place," Lord of lords means
"supreme Lord," and so on.

12

THE VISIONS
OF THE SEERS

Daniel and Revelation

T HERE ARE LINKS BETWEEN PROPHECY on one hand and
  Daniel and Revelation on the other. Daniel can be described
as a prophet (Mt 24:15), and Revelation refers to itself as a
prophecy (Rev 1:3). Nevertheless the book of Daniel and the
Revelation to John are so different from the works of the
prophets (and from other parts of both Old and New Testaments)
that they deserve to be looked at separately from them. The
aspects in which they are distinctive are the ones where they
have points of contact with each other.

These distinguishing features are of two kinds. One is the way
the two writers express themselves. Their teaching comes predominantly in the form of the report of visions, which suggests
a claim to have received their teaching direct from God. Many
believers since biblical times, and many non-Christians, have
claimed to have had visions, and there is no reason to say that
all of these must have been the product of overfertile imagina-
tions. Nowadays, scientists are less inclined to be dismissive of

psychic or extrasensory phenomena than was once the case, and particular examples need to be looked at on their merits. Prophets and apostles also tell of their visions (e.g., Zechariah, Paul in 2 Corinthians 12). But these experiences are not as prominent there as they are in Daniel and Revelation.

Hardly anything in these visions is expressed in a straightforward way. History after Daniel's time is related in code and symbol. Revelation describes heaven with its thrones, with the lamb in the center, with its temple, altar, and worshipers; calamity to come is described in terms of animals arising from the sea and bowls pouring out plagues. Frequently it is difficult to know where literal description ends and where symbolism begins, and to see what the symbols mean. The difficulty of understanding what Revelation signifies by the beast or the thousand-year reign of Jesus has led to the formulation of many different theories about their right interpretation.

The second type of distinctive feature in the visions in Daniel and Revelation lies in their actual beliefs and teaching. Each has a bleak view of the world and of history. The prophets assume that God is at work within history and that he fulfills his purpose by means of the decisions made by kings and nations. Either God's people were obedient to God and doing well, or they were disobedient and in trouble. But in the periods to which the visions in Daniel and Revelation relate, history was not working out in this way. Daniel relates to the Maccabean period (second century BC), when the Jewish people had committed no gross sin but were oppressed by the Seleucid king Antiochus, who even prevented proper worship of Yahweh. Revelation addresses itself to the predicament of believers pressured and persecuted by the Roman Empire in the last part of the first century AD. In both periods, history seemed to be working against God's purpose, and the two authors see this world as dominated by evil powers. They believe God is ultimately in control, but that at the moment he is letting evil have its way. They assume, however, that the days of evil are numbered and that a day will come when God vindicates his people and establishes his rule.

A consequence of this context and this view is that Daniel and Revelation do not issue the same challenge to moral living that characterizes the prophets. The prophets believe that there is a link between how people behave and how history works out. Daniel and Revelation cannot see that this is the case in their day, and therefore they do not demand repentance and commitment to God's moral will with the urgency that appears in the prophets. On the other hand, they do deliver a strong challenge regarding personal faithfulness to God despite the pressures that a crisis brings upon people. Daniel makes this point by its stories, Revelation by its promises to "those who win the victory."

In Daniel and Revelation the supernatural world is more clearly characterized than it is in other parts of the Bible. As well as references to evil powers, there are many allusions to angels and spirits. This feature may in part reflect a special awareness of God's greatness. If God is so absolutely on high, then there is increasing interest in beings such as angels through whom he acts in the world.

To what did the visions in Daniel and Revelation refer? Broadly, two main views may be described. One is that the seer is describing events that are to come centuries (even millennia) after his time, leading up to the end of the world. Daniel is then living in the exile but declaring what is to happen over the following centuries up to the Maccabees, and looking beyond that to the coming of Jesus and his second coming. Revelation is describing in outline the epochs of history that are to follow from the coming of Jesus to his second coming and the end of the world.

The second view is that the authors are people with a message for their own day. Thus the author of Daniel is living in the Maccabean period. Describing history from the exile onwards as if he were predicting the future is a dramatic device. He is thereby assuring his contemporaries that God really is in control of their destinies, by suggesting that history has been working out in a way controlled by God. Similarly, throughout the book of Revelation John is describing not events of the distant future but the crisis of the present and declaring that God is in control and is bringing the consummation of his purpose.

I think the second view makes more sense and is more of a piece with the way other parts of the Bible speak.

DANIEL

The visions in the book of Daniel begin with the period of the exile, the time of Daniel himself, when Nebuchadnezzar and the Babylonians controlled the people's destiny. They go on to the Maccabean period, when Antiochus Epiphanes and the Seleucids ruled Palestine (see chap. 2). The details of Daniel's visions are strange and puzzling, but the main drift is clear. Each speaks to the people of God in the terrible crisis that the oppression of Antiochus brought. They declare that the events of history, including such a crisis, are in God's control. These events are foreseen by him; they do not surprise him. He knows how long he is going to let the crisis last and how he is going to bring it to an end (see table 13.1). And the Jews did see Antiochus off.

Table 13.1. A key to the visions in Daniel

	Chapter 2	Chapter 7	Chapter 8	Chapter 9	Chapters 10–12
Babylonians	gold	lion/eagle	—	7 times 7 years	—
Medes and Persians	silver then bronze	bear then leopard	ram with two horns		five kings
Greeks (a) Alexander's empire	iron	horned beast	goat with prominent horn	7 times 62 years	mighty king of Greece
(b) empire divided	iron and clay feet	ten horns	four horns		breaking of his kingdom battles— Egypt and Syria
(c) Antiochus		little horn	little horn	3.5 years of horror	King of Syria dies
God's act (a) destruction	stone strikes iron and clay feet	beast killed	last king destroyed	horror ends	
(b) new act	stone becomes mountain	empire given to human figure		Israelites saved, dead rise	

Nebuchadnezzar the Babylonian emperor, along with Cyrus the Persian and other sixth-century figures, are named in connection with some of the visions. Antiochus is not named, but his actions are particularly clearly referred to in Daniel 11–12. This last vision gives a detailed summary of the history of the Greek period up to Antiochus's attempt to put an end to the Jews' worship of their God, though it does not name any of the figures. Instead they are simply referred to as "the king of Syria," "the king of Egypt," and so on. The vision then promises that God will intervene in this "time of trouble" and bring judgment and resurrection. Three and a half years (seven is a symbolic perfect number, and the figure represents half of this) will elapse before this deliverance: in other words, the period of oppression is limited and within God's control.

The same kind of reckoning appears in the previous vision (Dan 9), which follows a prayer of confession on Daniel's part on behalf of his people. The temple sacrifices are to be suspended by an invading king for three and a half years at the end of a period of seventy times seven years (approximately the time from the exile to the Maccabees). But then the invader will be dealt with.

This crisis in Jerusalem caused by Antiochus is described by the vision in Daniel 8, where the protagonists are identified as the various horns of a ram. Here the period of oppression is 1,150 days—again, a period of rather more than three years. This vision, too, promises that the affliction will be supernaturally ended.

The first two visions (Dan 2; 7) are similar to each other. In symbols they describe four successive empires, beginning with the Babylonians. They concentrate on the fourth empire, however, which at least in Daniel 7 (to judge from the parallels with the other visions) is again that ruled by Antiochus. Once more this empire is marvelously ended after three and a half years (Dan 7:25). Distinctive to the vision in Daniel 7 is the figure like a human being (Dan 7:13) to whom sovereignty is given after the fourth empire's fall. This figure represents the people of God (Dan 7:27). The symbol became important in later Jewish writings, and it is taken up as a title for Jesus himself (see, for instance, Mk 2:28; it is often translated by the cryptic phrase "Son of Man").

REVELATION

Revelation begins with letters to seven churches in the province of Asia (modern Turkey), challenging them about their faithfulness and promising God's own faithfulness to people who are really committed to him. Then the visions proper begin. First they describe a scene in heaven, where God is enthroned, surrounded by his heavenly worshipers. He holds a scroll with seven seals; it contains an outline of history, which is under his control. But who can be allowed to open the scroll? A "lamb standing in the center of the throne"—a lamb that "appeared to have been killed" (Jesus)—is declared worthy to do so, and thus the unveiling can begin. Ironically, it seems to conceal at the same time as it reveals, for although one can describe the contents, it is much more difficult to be sure what they mean.

The scroll tells of seven calamities that befall the earth (Rev 4–7). The first of these, such as war, are caused by human beings, but the later ones are "natural" disasters such as earthquakes. The sequence is relieved only by the picture of a vast multitude that is protected from the calamities by the lamb. The seventh seal unfolds a second sequence of seven "natural" disasters, heralded by means of trumpets blown by angels (Rev 8–11). This sequence ends with the power to rule over the world belonging to our Lord and his Messiah.

The most bizarre of the visions now follows (Rev 12–14), with extraordinary scenes describing a dragon that seeks to devour a newborn child, and grotesque beasts arising from earth and sea. On behalf of the dragon (which explicitly symbolizes the devil), the beasts compete with God for the allegiance of human beings. The lamb and his 144,000 followers stand, however, and the visions promise that God will judge the powers of evil and their followers. The features of the visions here are reminiscent of those in Daniel, though the detail is more developed.

The story is not over. The visions now describe seven plagues, "the final expression of God's wrath," further "natural" calamities bringing God's judgment on the beast (Rev 15). After these plagues, we read a description of the downfall of "the great whore," Babylon, which represents Rome, "the great city that rules over the kings of the earth" (Rev 17:18). God's people are challenged not to defile themselves by being involved with her. As a further encouragement to that end, Revelation closes with much more attractive pictures of the lamb's marriage feast, the death of the beast, the defeat of Satan, the new heaven and earth, the new Jerusalem, and the promise that Jesus is coming again (Rev 21–22).

In my opinion, two principles are worth bearing in mind as we read through this puzzling book. The first is that Revelation had a message for its own day. The book declares that the oppressive and persecuting Roman Empire (and the other persecutors of the church) will not have the last word; God will. Many of the features of the visions need to be understood against the background of the Roman Empire.

Yet the other principle is that the Roman Empire becomes a symbol of something bigger: it is the very embodiment of the powers of evil asserted against the purpose of God and the people of God. The significance of the book thus points beyond one particular historical situation, because it promises that God is the Lord who deals with any such self-assertive power. History is in God's control. The slain lamb holds the world's destiny. Thus, finally the book points us to the day when God will finally bring his "new Jerusalem," a vision for the future that is offered as an inspiration to people who worship God and the lamb, to encourage them to remain faithful despite suffering in the present.

The vision of a thousand-year reign of Christ, which comes toward the end of the book but just before these final chapters

(Rev 20), has been regarded as of great significance as a portrayal of the "millennium," usually regarded as an age of great blessing still to come and preceding the final consummation of God's purpose. This chapter is the Bible's only reference to such a millennium, and the characteristic ambiguity of Revelation's symbolism has led to wide disagreement as to what the millennium means. It is unwise to base too much on this chapter because we cannot be sure how the picture given there is meant to relate to other pictures in the book.

PART IV

ISRAEL'S RESPONSE TO GOD

T HERE IS A SENSE IN WHICH THE WHOLE BIBLE is Israel's response to what God has done and to how he has spoken. But there are some parts in which this response is overtly expressed. The book of Psalms contains psalms of praise and thanksgiving as the writer contemplates God's character and actions. There are also the psalms of prayer and protest which (along with Lamentations) are Israel's response to God when he seems to allow calamity to befall it.

In two other Old Testament books, however, Ecclesiastes and Job, it is not the voice of faith but the voice of doubt that is dominant. The Bible includes in its library that genuinely human voice; it accepts the possibility of questioning God.

13

PRAYER AND PRAISE

Psalms and Lamentations

L IKE OUR HYMNS, the psalms express their praise in poetry.
Unlike most of our hymns, they do not have regular
numbers of syllables in a line or use rhyme. Most verses have
two halves, and the halves complement each other in some way.
They may say similar things twice in different words:

Come, let's shout to Yahweh: let's call out to the rock who
delivers us. (Ps 95:1)

Or they may make two converse statements:

They call on chariots, they call on horses: but we call on the
name of Yahweh our God. (Ps 20:7)

Or the second half may simply complete the first, clarifying it or
making it more specific or taking its thought further:

I will study the way of the upright: when shall I reach it?
(Ps 101:2)

In one way or another, the one-line verse is thus usually the unit
of thought.

Within each line, there is commonly a regular number of words, though this is not obvious in English, because Hebrew strings together as one word what would be several words in English. In the Hebrew there are most often three words in each line, and in English you can often spot how it works by looking for the important words:

Come, let's-shout to-Yahweh: let's-call-out to-the-rock who-delivers-us. (Ps 95:1)

In more prayerful psalms, there can sometimes be only two words in the second half—this gives more of a limping lilt to the poetry:

Listen-to my-words, Yahweh: consider my-sighs.
Listen-to my-cry for-help: my-God and-king. (Ps 5:1-2)

The verses don't consistently work out as neatly as this example; often there can be more words in the line. We don't know how the psalms were originally sung, but I think of the psalms as like rap music—you can have varying numbers of words in the line as long as you keep the rhythm going.

Psalms begin with introductions. Many are notes indicating where the psalm came from: "a poem of the sons of Korah" (e.g., Ps 44) was one in the hymnbook of the Korahites, and so on. Others give directions for the use of the psalm or for its musical accompaniment. Many of these introductions are puzzling. Several refer to incidents in David's life, but most psalms give no hint when they were written. We may make guesses as to the historical circumstances that produced a particular psalm, but these are only guesses. We can be more certain, in a general sense, of the circumstances in which the psalms were used once they had been written. The book of Psalms is Israel's hymnbook and prayer book; a hymnbook and prayer book is most at home in church, and the book of Psalms is the hymnbook of the temple.

The temple was the center of religious faith for Israelites to a greater extent than a church is for Christians—at least for people who lived in Jerusalem. God had promised Israel that they would know his presence in the temple. This presence is often expressed in terms of his "name" being there. The Israelites knew that God himself in his totality could not be in the temple—the whole heaven was not large enough to hold him, so how could a humanly made building (1 Kings 8:27)? But Israel knew God's name. If you address someone by name it means you are on good terms with the person. A name may indeed express something about the hopes the parents had for their child. Hebrew names sometimes expressed a person's character or destiny. "Adam" was made of earth (Hebrew *adamah* [see Gen 2:7]), "Abraham" suggested the phrase "father of many nations" (see Gen 17:5), Solomon's reign was characterized by peace and prosperity (*shalom* [see 1 Chron 22:9]).

The distinctive name of Israel's God was Yahweh. It doesn't mean "the Lord," as it usually appears in translations. It is God's personal name, revealed to Israel. This name, too, has implications: it resembles the verb "to be." The name Yahweh suggests the one who is there, the one who makes his presence felt (see chap. 4). So Israel knew God's name, was on personal-name terms with God, and knew something of his character. When people uttered God's name it expressed the awareness that God was present. Because the temple was the place where Yahweh's name was declared in worship, the temple was the place where his presence was known. It was thus the center of Israel's spiritual life. Nation and individuals came here at moments of joy and in times of crisis (as Samuel, Kings, and Chronicles show) to bring their praise and prayer. The book of Psalms is a collection of these praises and prayers.

Like the messages of the prophets, the psalms have various types of outward shape and form, and it helps us if we can see what different examples of each type of psalm have in common and how the types differ from each other. Comparing examples of the same type both helps to understand what all these examples meant to Israel and enables us to appreciate what may be their individually distinctive features.

The different types illustrate different ways of speaking to God. The kind of basic exclamations human beings make to one another, such as "please," "help," "sorry," "thank you," "that's great," "you're great," "I love you," are the fundamental things people say to God, too.

PLEASE, HELP, SORRY

Often the psalms express human need. Some are the prayers of the whole people, apparently gathered in the temple in some national crisis. Psalm 74, for instance, describes the devastation wrought by enemies and pleads with God to do something about it. Psalm 60 similarly speaks of the land falling apart because God has let the nation be defeated. Toward the end of this psalm, however, an "I" speaks: "Who, O God, will take me into the fortified city? Who will lead me to Edom?" Presumably here the king, as Israel's leader in battle, speaks. The king would be prominent in the people's worship, especially on an occasion of national crisis or national rejoicing.

It makes sense to see many other psalms that speak simply of "I" as similarly uttered by the king, or uttered on his behalf, on such occasions of crisis or celebration. Such psalms as Psalms 3; 5; 25, then, exemplify the prayer of the nation's leader when the nation is under pressure.

Other "I" psalms show less indication of being the prayers of a leader, and these are more likely provided for the use of ordinary individuals. They may be the protest of someone oppressed by the wicked, or a sick person's prayer for healing, or a sinner's plea for forgiveness: indeed these motifs may be interwoven (e.g., Pss 38; 39; 41).

Presumably in such situations individuals would ideally come (perhaps with their family and friends) to the temple to pray, if they lived in Jerusalem, and these are the psalms they would use. Other "I" psalms may be intended for the whole congregation to use. An example outside the book of Psalms is Lamentations 3, a prayer like the others in Lamentations that was written for the people to use after the destruction of Jerusalem but that speaks of "I."

Although these prayers came out of diverse background situations, there are certain elements in them that tend to recur.

1. *This is how things are and how I feel.* After an introduction calling on God that introduces the prayer, the feature that dominates these prayers (in the sense that it occupies most verses) is the description of the person's need, in the form of a protest at the suffering or oppression he or she is undergoing. The psalm describes this affliction at some length, no doubt in part as a way of getting it off the chest to God (who is the one who can do something about it). The experience of affliction may be described from three perspectives: the psalm speaks of "they/he," "we/I," and "you." It

thus speaks of the undeserved hostility and deceit that *other people* have shown; of the loneliness and oppression that *the person* feels; and, worst of all, of how *God* has let the person down.

2. *This is why you should respond to my prayer.* The psalms commonly go on from their protest to express, nevertheless, trust in God to respond to the person praying in his or her need, continuing to believe that God alone can rescue and restore. These statements provide a further reason why God should answer the prayer, but in these declarations of praise to God and trust in him, we can also hear people reassuring themselves and seeking to build up the trust that present experience seems to belie. As well as confessing trust in God, the psalms sometimes also confess sin against God: their acknowledgment of sin clears the way to God's forgiveness and restoration. More often, people protest that they have *not* acted wrongly, that it cannot be said that the misfortune that has come upon them is what they deserve. They have been faithful to God; the trouble is, God has not been faithful to them. So again, they urge God to respond, by denying that their sin is a reason why God should not be faithful. Clearly the claim not to have sinned could be arrogant—and is arrogant, if they are implying that they have never done anything wrong. But they are rather saying that they have not gone back on their commitment to God in such a way as to deserve the kind of affliction they are experiencing.

3. *So this is what I ask for.* The psalm's actual prayer is a relatively short section in the psalm as a whole. Indeed, even the prayer part is not very specific—there is no list of precise requests.

It may be summed up in a phrase such as "Rescue me" or simply "Do something." Or the aspects of affliction described earlier are picked up in the prayer. With respect to God, the psalm prays that he may turn in love to his servant, instead of seeming to have his face turned away; and that he may intervene in the situation, instead of seeming to do nothing. With respect to the enemies, it may pray that they may be confuted and that judgment may come on them in turn. With respect to the individual, the psalm may pray for healing, victory, or restoration.

4. *God will answer me!* In many psalms there is a change of mood before the end: the psalm begins to speak as if the prayer has been answered (see, for example, the transition in Psalm 28 between verses 5 and 6). This may sometimes simply express the assurance that God does hear prayer and therefore that the burden has been passed over to God. But on some occasions, at this point in the psalm the suppliant may have been verbally assured by a priest or prophet that God had heard and would respond. (See the messages incorporated into Psalms 12; 60.) It is to this assurance that the psalm then responds in praise as its mood changes. The note of praise appears frequently in these prayers that arise out of need. It commonly closes the psalm. As the psalm looks forward to God answering the prayer, it looks in anticipatory praise even beyond that to the privilege, responsibility, and joy of returning to the temple to give public acknowledgment of the grace and power of the God who has responded to the prayer.

LAMENTATIONS

The five poems that make up Lamentations are examples of such prayers, examples deriving from one particular disaster, the destruction of Jerusalem in 587. In describing how *I feel*, they give us a description of the sufferings and sorrows of the experience: the desolation of the city that God had said he would protect and where he had lived in the temple, the gloating of Israel's enemies, the degradation of the people (women eating their dead babies), the abandonment and anger of God himself. The five poems each have twenty-two units, twenty-two being the number of letters in the Hebrew alphabet, and in Lamentations 1–4 each unit begins with a different letter of the alphabet: they are expressions of grief from A to Z.

So *why should God respond to their prayer?* Lamentations acknowledges that the affliction was deserved. The people had been unfaithful to God, and here they confess that the punishment that has come upon them is deserved. They have no claims on God. If God answers (Lamentations acknowledges it is a big *if*), it will be because of his mercy, not their rights. Their only hope is his "unfailing love and mercy" (Lam 3:22).

What they ask for is for a time when God, in this unfailing love, "looks down from heaven and sees us" (Lam 3:50). "Bring us back to you, Yahweh! Bring us back! Restore our ancient glory" (Lam 5:21). Combined with this plea is a recurrent appeal to God, in all justice, to punish their attackers as he has punished them.

The conviction that God *will answer me* is not as confidently expressed as it is in the Psalms. Lamentations still believes God does answer (see Lam 3:55-60). But the poems end with a question rather than a statement, "Or have you rejected us forever?" (Lam 5:22). The people deserve no more, they know, and too fervent a conviction would belie their confession of sin.

THANK YOU, THAT'S GREAT, YOU'RE GREAT, I LOVE YOU

Thank you. The prayers in the psalms look forward to thanksgiving and praise; naturally there are also therefore psalms that express thanksgiving for God's response to prayer. These also belong to the temple, but the feelings they express do not have their origin there. The psalm is the formalizing of a response one naturally makes at the moment of Yahweh's act. We can sometimes trace this response in the Old Testament's narratives of events. When God answered Israel's prayer by taking them through the Reed Sea and enabling them to escape from their pursuers, "the prophet Miriam, Aaron's sister, took her tambourine, and all the women followed her, playing tambourines and dancing. Miriam sang for them: Sing to Yahweh, because he has won a glorious victory, he has thrown the horses and their riders into the sea" (Ex 15:20-21).

Praise begins in life. But then people who have had their prayer answered come before God and his people to say so. Merely giving thanks in private would not be enough; God deserves public acknowledgment for what he has done, and the psalms are glad to offer it. In their protests people promise to come back to praise God for answering their prayer, and now they do so.

The thanksgiving itself is essentially a grateful look back, with several natural elements. The psalm recalls the predicament the person had been in—the physical and emotional distress, the threat of death itself, and the feeling of the absence and neglect of God. It recalls the urgent plea made to God in this situation. With joy it recalls how God did exactly as the psalm asked. God, whose face had seemed hidden and uncaring, turned to the person; then God acted to restore physical and emotional well-being and the joy and praise that are supposed to characterize an Israelite's life. But as the prayers talk not so much about how I think God should act as about what are the facts he should do something about, so the thanksgivings talk not so much about grateful feelings but about the facts the person can feel grateful about.

This praise the psalmist promises to continue to offer, not merely for God's responses to particular prayers but for all that God has done and that God is for his people, all that of which this recent experience of God's grace has given the psalmist a fresh conviction.

That's great. As the prayers lead logically to the thanksgivings, the thanksgivings lead logically to the psalms of praise. The difference is that the psalms of praise do not have a particular recent experience to rejoice in; they have more permanent things in mind.

Sometimes this praise is indirect: God is praised by glorying in what belongs to him, what he has made, what he gives. One theme that comes over particularly prominently is God's activity as Lord of creation. God's sovereignty as Creator lies behind both his sovereignty in history (on which "the story of God and his people" concentrates) and his sovereignty in personal experience (of which the prayers and thanksgivings speak).

Creation, as the psalms rejoice in it, is not merely the long-ago past event that set the world going. It is God's present activity. God ensures that the powers of chaos cannot reassert themselves;

the world is secure. God makes the rain fall and the grass grow: God thus feeds human beings and animals. The cosmos declares his glory. Psalm 19, one that does rejoice in God's creation, goes on to add a note of praise to God for his word. A lyrical joy in God's word appears in several psalms, most systematically in Psalm 119.

The Psalms also rejoice in Jerusalem and its temple. Other peoples had their sacred city, their sacred hill, their sacred building. The Psalms know that Jerusalem is the true center of the world, because it is the city God chose; Mount Zion is the real mountain of God, despite its physical insignificance. The temple there is the true dwelling place of God Almighty.

So God is praised not only directly, by acknowledging him, but by saying "that's great" with regard to the world he creates, the word he utters, and the city he inhabits. As long as none of these come to be rejoiced in independently of him, all is well.

You're great. There are further psalms that rejoice in God himself, describe his character and his deeds, and make that a reason for praising him. They begin by calling people to praise: the whole world should be involved for this praise to be worthy of God, but often the psalm is satisfied to call on all Israel. This invitation or challenge is backed up by the reasons for it, which arise out of God's character. These reasons may be summed up in short phrases. They may be amplified by some rejoicing in how God has revealed himself in his characteristic areas of activity: in creation, in the great historical events such as the exodus that established Israel as a nation, and in the providence God exercises in the everyday lives of people and in the situations that confront Israel.

CREEDS, BLESSINGS, PROMISES, CHALLENGES

While the Psalms are dominated by prayer and praise, they have some other aspects. They begin with a blessing (Ps 1) that describes the protection and prosperity God gives those who are committed to him. This is not the only psalm that brings a challenge: Psalm 15 and Psalm 24, for instance, remind the worshiper of the moral qualities that must characterize people who come into God's presence. Psalm 50 and Psalm 82 go beyond that reminder in declaring God's judgment on injustice. Nor is Psalm 1 the only one that declares the psalmist's own creed: Psalm 37, for instance, speaks of a conviction with regard to God's faithfulness, while Psalm 49 proclaims a belief that God will even rescue from death.

After the blessing comes a promise concerning the king (Ps 2), and here a major theme of the psalms is introduced. The "I" of the psalms is often that of the king. Here the Psalms' concern with the king is explicit. God promises his commitment to the king, because the king is the means of God's lordship being exercised in the world. There are several psalms that speak of varied aspects of the king's significance: Psalm 72 prays for his fulfillment of the role of bringing justice; Psalm 89 recalls the promise made to David and asks for its fulfillment now; Psalm 45 prays for blessing on his marriage; and so on. These psalms for the king came to be interpreted messianically—that is, they came to express the hope that one day Israel would be given a king who would really live up to the theology of kingship expressed here. They thus come to be applied to Jesus in the New Testament. But they were written with real present kings of David's line in Jerusalem in mind. They challenge them to live up to the kingly ideal and promise them God's commitment as they seek to do so.

14

DOUBTS AND CERTAINTIES

Ecclesiastes and Job

I T IS SLIGHTLY ARBITRARY TO TREAT ECCLESIASTES and Job in a different chapter from Proverbs, because these two books also embody the approach to life of Israel's scholars, and they too are meant as teaching—in this sense they belong to "The word of God to his people." But they are books that speak *to* God as much as *about* God, yet with a very different accent from the voice that praises God in the Psalms. Admittedly the Psalms are often lamenting God's absence; and Ecclesiastes may be seen as taking to greater length the questioning of the point of everything, which appears (for instance) in Psalm 49 and Psalm 73. Job, in turn, has many features that suggest an extended protest psalm.

ECCLESIASTES

Ecclesiastes has been described as the most modern book in the Bible. It takes up many of the concerns of contemporary Western society—freedom, justice, pleasure, success, progress, money, knowledge, ambition, power, sex—and asks what they are really worth and whether they can make life worthwhile. The answer is a clear no. The point is plain as the book begins, because it announces its theme in its opening lines: "It is empty, empty, said the churchman. Life is empty, all empty." *Empty* is a key word in the book. It also means "a breath"—something that has no body to it, a mere puff of wind.

The fundamental reason why life is empty is that death hangs over it: death, which despite all our efforts we can't avoid; death, which is so unfair, cutting off in their prime people who ought to live long and happy lives (and ignoring people whose wrongdoing makes them deserve to die); death, which is unpredictable, so that a people can never know when their day will come, and thus plan for it; death, which is above all unpleasant. Not that Ecclesiastes (or other parts of the Old Testament) saw in death the flames of hell causing perpetual torment. Death just meant an end to all the good things: your body was stuck in a dark rock tomb to rot, and your personality joined the other pathetic personalities in Sheol, the home of the dead. It was a place characterized by what you couldn't do: there, Ecclesiastes says, there is no doing, no feeling, no thought, no knowledge, no wisdom, no reward, no acknowledgment, and no hope (Eccles 9:5-6, 10). The most striking thing about death must be its boredom.

So what attitude are we to take to life? There are two attitudes that Ecclesiastes rejects. One is the indulgence in activity and achievement that hides from the truth of the human situation. That is escapism. The other is the pie-in-the-sky solution that asserts, hopefully, that all will be put right after death. "After all," says Ecclesiastes, "the same fate awaits human being and animal alike. One dies just like the other. They are both going to the same place—the dust. How can anyone be sure that a human being's spirit goes upwards while an animal's spirit goes down to the ground?" (Eccles 3:19-21). (In the light of Jesus' resurrection, of course, there is more to be said.)

There is another possible response, which Ecclesiastes does not consider: wouldn't it be logical to commit suicide? An intuition tells us not, but why not? I think Ecclesiastes's answer would be the fact that we receive life as a gift from God, so it is not for us to spurn it or decide for ourselves when the spirit God gives is to be returned to him. This fact, that it is God who gives life, is a fundamental conviction that forms Ecclesiastes's own attitude to life. We can't understand the big questions, we can't achieve the big things we'd love to strive for. But the fact remains that we receive life from the Creator himself, and although he remains an enigma, the personal, everyday satisfactions of food and drink, work and personal relationships, may be received and enjoyed as God's gifts. They are not to be treated as ultimate ends in themselves, nor devoured with the despair or abandon of "Let us eat, drink, and be merry, for tomorrow we die," but received humbly, seriously, yet joyfully, as things God has given; we must just accept the absence of what he has not given.

JOB

What is the book of Job about? The obvious answer is, it's about the problem of suffering, and it has a great deal to teach us about that topic. But why does it discuss the problem of suffering? The real concern of the book of Job is the question "What kind of relationship is there between us and God, and how do we live our lives and live with suffering in light of the answer to those questions?" It discusses the problem of suffering because Job's suffering makes Job into a test case with regard to this question. Job doesn't give you an "answer" to the problem of suffering.

We noted in chapter eleven that Israel's experts and scholars sought to instruct Israel in what attitudes to life worked. They believed that a righteous life was also a sensible life; God made life work in such a way that a moral life was also a happy and successful one. The belief may be true much of the time, but it is not always true; and what attitude do you take to the exceptions?

To let goodness be seen to be rewarded flaunts before us the temptation to be good for what we can get out of it: to turn the relationship between us and God into a commercial one. Commercial relationships have their place: business depends on people agreeing to give something in return for something else. In these relationships, our own interest, what we can get out of it, is uppermost in our mind. But we recognize that there is something more profound, more human, about the personal relationships in which people give to one another without thought for what they will get in return—when they keep on loving even when their love is spurned, when they demonstrate that "love never gives up; its faith, hope, and patience never fail" (1 Cor 13:7).

Which kind of relationship obtains between us and God? Job was a man who had proved that morality, conformity, and religion paid dividends (Job 1:1-3). He was a model of piety and life. But was he religious only because it paid? This was the "accuser's" explanation (Job 1:8-10: the word for "accuser" or "adversary" is often transliterated as "Satan," but in the Old Testament *satan* is an ordinary Hebrew word for "opponent," not a proper name, and this "adversary" is not the great prince of darkness). Perhaps Job is only in it for what he can get out of it. And perhaps God only cultivates human adulation because he is lonely or it boosts his ego. Perhaps he is like the big boy who desperately needs to impress the little boys. Perhaps the whole relationship between God and us is a sham. It looks from the outside like one of love and trust, but really it's only "scratch my back and I'll scratch yours," not a personal relationship but a commercial one.

How is it to be established whether God or the accuser is right? In a business relationship, if one party withdraws, the other party has the right to do so too. If you do not renew your subscription to your automobile association, the service truck will not be available. If God withdraws his blessing from Job, will he still be uniquely blameless and upright, God-fearing and righteous?

See table 15.1 for an outline of the book.

Table 15.1. A basic outline of Job

The basic story	The argument between Job and his friends	Some sidebars
1–2 Beginning	3 Job's complaints	
	4–14 First round	
	15–21 Second round	
	22–27 Third round	
		28 Poem praising wisdom
	29–31 Job's final statement	
		32–37 Elihu's speeches
	38–42:6 Yahweh responds	
42:7-17 Ending		

After the introduction, the scenes that follow in Job's story show his life falling apart. He loses his possessions in a series of business calamities (Job 1:14-17). He loses his sons and daughters in a natural disaster (Job 1:18-19). He loses his health (Job 2:7-8), his wife despairs (Job 2:9), and his friends—who assume that the business relationship picture is the right one—conclude that he must have broken his side of the bargain, and berate him accordingly (Job 4–27).

The drama opens up many questions other than the one from which the story starts. Job's own spiritual pilgrimage takes him along ways he could not have dreamed of. His relationship with God undergoes the severest strains, and his assertiveness has to be rebuked. But the adversary had predicted he would curse God, and his wife had urged him to do so. His friends had tried to browbeat him into confessing sins he had not committed. These things he did not do. And at the end of the story he is commended—he had spoken the truth (Job 42:7)—and he is given new blessings. He never knew (as far as the story tells us) the reason for his experience. But the relationship was vindicated.

What insights on the problem of suffering are suggested by all this? In the course of the testing of the relationship between Job and God, the question of suffering is approached from various angles. Job's three friends assume that Job suffers because of his sin. This assumption was one that came naturally to them: it was what "the advice of the scholars" taught. It was a truth that had proved itself over the generations; it was what orthodoxy had always taught, as Bildad especially emphasized. It was also the truth maintained by Eliphaz, though he adds an extra ground for accepting it: he has received a supernatural revelation concerning the matter (Job 4:12-21).

There is truth in this view. There is a connection between sin and suffering. It is true in a general sense—the amount of suffering in the world is at least in part to be explained as in various senses the result of human sin. And it is often true in detail with regard to particular situations. (Paul, for instance, attributes certain illnesses and deaths among the Corinthians to their failure to "recognize the meaning of the Lord's body" at the Lord's Supper [1 Cor 11:29-30]). But Job receives a disproportionate share of the general suffering in the world, and he is not a notorious sinner. The theory does not cover him—unless the story of his life is first rewritten to include many sins (as it is, by the friends).

Elihu, the angry young man who appears toward the end of the debate (Job 32–37), suggests a variation on this theme. Elihu is the great champion of human reason: he believes that God gave us our minds and that we can find answers if we will use our minds. Suffering, he declares, can be intended to bring us back to God. It is thus an expression of God's loving concern for his creatures. Again, this approach is biblical, but somehow not quite relevant: Job is a committed believer, so hardly in need of such chastening.

The opening of the book suggests that Job's suffering is sent as a test. This view, too, can be paralleled elsewhere in the Bible (e.g., 1 Pet 1:7). But even this answer is irrelevant to the question, how is Job to cope with suffering, because Job is not told that this was the explanation. Job never gets an answer to his question *why*, even though he could have been given one.

Job's attitude is commended at the end of the story, because he had at least insisted on facing facts—unlike his friends, who rewrote the facts and made Job into a sinner in order that he could fit into their theories. Nevertheless, he is not meekly accepting of what he has to go through. On the contrary, as he gets more and more annoyed with his friends, so he becomes more and more insistent that God is being unreasonable, and more and more determined to clear his name. If necessary, he will be satisfied if this clearing of his name comes only after his death: envisaging this possibility, Job comes out with his famous "I know that my redeemer liveth"

(Job 16:18-22; 19:23-27). But vindication and release after death are second best to the vindication he demands now.

Before Job's final review of his former happiness, present misery, and lifelong righteous conduct (Job 29–31), there appears a poem about God's unfathomable wisdom (Job 28). It offers a comment on the debate, which conveys an implicit judgment on both Job and his friends. They think they have the truth all tied up, but they are wrong. Job sees that point and wants to go beyond them. He thinks he is entitled to know the truth, but he is wrong too. God's wisdom is unfathomable; the poem ends with the reminder that recurs through the wisdom books, that the humble worship of God provides the only starting point for beginning to understand his ways. The poem raises issues that will be taken further when God appears to Job.

When this happens, God in a sense grants Job the confrontation he has asked for. But Job finds the occasion is not one on which he is confronting God; it is God confronting him. It is God who asks the questions, not Job. The questions involve a conducted tour of creation, in the course of which God keeps asking, "Could you do that? Were you there when I made that? Can your mind understand that? Can you see that this creation does not revolve around you?" The purpose of the confrontation is to drive home a point that has been made in earlier speeches, though not with such force. God is the Lord of creation, and it is impossible for humanity to question him or to aspire to understanding his purpose in its totality. Job must not protest as if he is the center of the world. The world is much bigger than him.

Job is prepared to grant the point (Job 40:1-5), but when he does so, God does not stop questioning him. The confrontation resumes, and here centers on the question, what can Job do about the unfairness and injustice that often characterizes human life? Job complains about injustice, but he cannot himself do anything to lessen the element of unfairness in human experience. Having challenged him on this point, God points to two huge and frightening creatures, Behemoth and Leviathan. In the myths of Middle Eastern peoples, they epitomized the power of evil and chaos asserted against goodness and order. (In fact, *they* are the equivalent to Satan.) But they are under God's control; they are, in fact, only animals (Israel's equivalent to the Loch Ness Monster: theoretically fearsome, but in practice the object of fun). There are no powers of chaos and injustice beyond God's control. The very creation shows that God's power and wisdom rule the world.

Job had been questioning whether justice and providence were in control in the world, because in his own personal world they did not seem to be so. The person who suffers is challenged to believe, despite his suffering, that God's power and wisdom do rule. How his present experience fits in, Job cannot see and God does not explain. But creation shows that God can be trusted, even where he cannot be understood.

The book, then, accompanies doubts with certainties. The Bible as a whole does not claim to answer every question: some questions have to be left to the mystery of God. But it does claim that in light of creation (and of the story of Israel and the story of the cross) there are enough certainties for us to carry on trusting even where we cannot understand.

EPILOGUE

The Bible Today

W E HAVE BEEN ATTEMPTING to understand the Bible for what it meant to the people who wrote it and the people for whom it was written, as we might investigate the writings of the Greeks or the Quran. In the introduction, we noted that in order to appreciate the Bible, we had to take up a sympathetic approach to it. Whether or not we believe in God, we are trying to get inside the thinking of people who did believe in God. We are unlikely to gain real insight into their writings if we cannot suspend our beliefs and disbeliefs while we try to understand theirs. No more is required than is needed if I try to read the Qur'an. If I am concerned only with proving it wrong, I will probably never understand. I have to aim to look at the world through its spectacles.

When I do so, I may find that I let myself in for more than I bargained for. Unless the book I'm trying to understand contains no sense at all, there are things I may learn from its insights. If I do manage to look at the world through its spectacles, I find that I am challenged to keep those spectacles on. In certain ways, I find that they have the world in focus. I can hardly then throw them away and resume looking at the world the way I did before.

If this is generally true about the sensitive reading of an important book, it certainly applies to the Bible, which pushes us to an attitude of more than mere curiosity. It claims to provide definitive insights on the most urgent questions faced by people in every age: What is human life about? Why is humanity's story such a puzzling combination of achievement and failure, goodness and badness, success and degradation? Where is the world going? Is there a God, and (if so) what is he like, and on what basis can we relate to him? What sort of life ought we to live, and how can we live up even to the standards we do see?

The Bible's response to these questions comes in the form of stories and statements and pictures. The statements give us answers to some of the questions. The stories help us understand the answers and tell us how God did what needed to be done for these answers to work. The pictures illustrate the answers.

The story comes to a climax in Jesus Christ. His death and resurrection made it possible for the relationship between humanity and God to be healed, and these events assure us that God is Lord of human history. Now we can enjoy the relationship that God intended for us from the beginning and begin to live life in this world to the full, as God intended.

The New Testament, then, tells us the final facts on which this life with God is based and tells us how it was worked out for the first Christian churches. Believers today cannot get away from the writings of the first believers, those who were nearest to the Jesus of history himself. And if we want to follow in their footsteps, then we can learn from their experiences, their problems, their insights.

We have to allow for the difference in situation between ourselves and the New Testament believers. We belong to a different age and a different culture. We are not necessarily superior to them, even though we are technologically more sophisticated. We too ask those perennial questions about life; the questions are largely timeless. We face the same questions about sin and goodness. But how we work out the implications of their answers, and how we express these answers in the language of our day, will vary.

The New Testament believers interpreted what Jesus' death means for the relationship between humanity and God by picking up human experiences of their day and using them as illustrations of what happens between God and us. What God has done for us in Jesus is like him paying the price for a slave's release from bondage (redemption), or like him offering a sacrifice in a temple to deal with something that has made a person unclean (expiation), or like him acquitting a person because someone else has paid the person's penalty (justification), or like him mediating between two people who have been at enmity with each other (reconciliation). Some of these pictures (probably the last two) can mean as much in our cultures today as they did in New Testament times. Others (maybe the first two) mean little in Western society. They need a lot of explanation before we can appreciate them. They also need to be supplemented by illustrations drawn from our everyday life, as Paul, for instance, drew them from his.

Again, the instructions that the New Testament gives are always related to the social conditions of the day. Usually this causes no problems: stealing and perjury are as wrong in our culture as they were in the first century. But at some points, social customs affect the validity of the instructions. The classic example is Paul's exhortation in 1 Corinthians 11 concerning the wearing of hats by Christian women. It seems that one reason Paul saw this as important is that in Corinth only women of loose morals appeared in public bare-headed. (We might compare the veiling accepted by Arab women today.) It would then be understandable that Paul does not want the Corinthian women, in parading their Christian freedom, to give the wrong impression. Today, however, putting on your best hat to go to church may be almost a symbol of hypocrisy; so in obeying Paul to the letter we may miss the spirit of what he was saying and in effect do the opposite of what he wanted.

On the other hand, we need to be wary of explaining away the teaching of the Bible by saying it was limited to its culture. More often than not, its teaching is applicable to our day in a straightforward way; the only question is whether we will accept it.

One further aspect of the challenge brought by the time gap and culture gap between the Bible and ourselves is the fact that often it does not address the precise problems with which we are concerned. It has lots to say about sexual morality—the only question, again, is whether we will accept it. It has nothing direct to say about conservation or genetic engineering (nothing direct, that is, though its understanding of God, humanity, and the world in a general sense will have implications for such questions). This means that believers cannot say, "I'll make sure I do all that the Bible says, and then I'll know I've fulfilled God's will." We have to do what the Bible says, but also ask what further theological and moral questions are raised by the world in which we live and the lives we have to live, and go on to ask, "If that was how God spoke to his people in their situation in the Bible, what may he be saying to us in ours?" And when people say, "This is what we believe God is calling us to do now," they will test such a claim by asking, "Is that the kind of thing that we would expect God to be saying, on the basis of what the Bible tells us he has already said and done?"

Western believers usually find that relating the New Testament to us is not so complicated (perhaps it is more complicated than they have thought). They have found the Old Testament more difficult to handle, and so we will spend the final section of this book looking in particular at the meaning of the Old Testament for today. We will do this by considering six ways in which believers may look at the Old Testament. There is value in each of them; different methods may be more illuminating when applied to different parts of the Old Testament.

1. THE OLD TESTAMENT IS THE BACKGROUND TO THE NEW TESTAMENT

We begin from the fact that Jesus cannot be understood without taking the Old Testament into account, because the Old Testament was Jesus' Bible.

One thing that struck people about Jesus was the fact that he spoke "with authority." He was not like teachers who debated and expounded the meaning of Scripture but would not dare to say anything on their own authority. Jesus spoke as a man in direct touch with God.

Despite this fact, the way Jesus does refer to the Scriptures is striking. From the beginning of his story in the New Testament we see how involved with the Scriptures he is. It is words from a psalm, from Genesis, and from Isaiah that address him at his baptism (Mt 3:17). It is commands from Deuteronomy that he quotes to the devil during his temptation (Mt 4:1-11). It is a prophecy in Isaiah that guides the direction of his ministry (Mt 4:12-17). His description of true happiness reflects the Psalms and Isaiah (Mt 5:3-8). He sums up his aim as to make the teachings of the Torah and Prophets come true; the smallest detail of the Torah will not be done away with (Mt 5:17-18). It is Matthew who makes this point most explicit. But his picture of Jesus' reliance on the Old Testament with regard to his theology, his living, his ministry, and his teaching is not essentially different from the one that pervades the Gospels.

It naturally follows that we can understand Jesus and the New Testament writers only if we understand the assumptions they make on the basis of the Old Testament. Jesus' mission, for instance, is spoken of in terms of the Messiah and the Son of Man, and the ultimate background of these titles lies in the Old Testament's hope of a kingly redeemer, a new David, or of a new man, such as the human figure in Daniel's vision (Dan 7). While the way the New Testament speaks of these figures also reflects Jewish thinking of later times, it is their presence in the Old Testament that makes these figures inevitable to the New Testament's understanding of Jesus. The Scriptures provide the framework for understanding Jesus. So we need the Old Testament to tell us how the New Testament saw the question to which Jesus was the answer. The Old Testament describes the problem and the way it needed to be solved: Jesus comes and declares himself to be the one to solve it.

2. The Old Testament Is an Incomplete Story

In describing the Old Testament as setting up the questions to which Jesus is the answer, we acknowledge that the Old Testament has no final answer to some of the questions it sets. It is open-ended.

The New Testament has several ways of taking up this fact. We may consider them by reviewing some of the sections of this book. First, as a story, the main account of the events from creation through the exodus and occupation of Palestine to the exile is a story with a dead end. God made the world, he tried to redeem the world, but he apparently failed. The second version of the story in Chronicles-Ezra-Nehemiah sets the story going again, but stops in the middle of things.

The teaching of the priests underlines the failure of what God has done so far. This teaching was given to Israel to obey, and obeying it was the key to being blessed by God. But the Torah itself recognizes that it will not be obeyed (see Deut 29–32).

The advice of the scholars is also incomplete. Proverbs and the Song of Songs give impressive descriptions of what life could be like, but Job and Ecclesiastes protest that the descriptions do not ring true; it is not what life actually is like. Here the questions about the meaning of human life are faced more radically than anywhere else in the Bible, but Job and Ecclesiastes are better at questions than answers and can only offer trust in the mystery of God.

The words of the prophets and the visions of the seers look beyond present failure to the glorious consummation of God's purpose. But the glorious consummation keeps being put off. Isaiah 40–55 pictures desert turned into pools of water, but the desert is not turned into pools of water. The picture of the whole world coming to acknowledge Yahweh does not find fulfillment.

The Old Testament recognizes the predicament from which humanity needed redemption. Every exposure of the depth of human failure can make us more appreciative of what God achieved in Christ.

At the same time, believers have to see themselves as potentially in the same position as Old Testament Israel. They cannot assume that Old Testament Israel was cast off forever, while the church has now taken its place. On the contrary, God still plans to save Israel, and if the church does not remain faithful, it can be cast off as Israel was (see Rom 11:22-27). So Israel's story is full of warnings for the church. Further, the New Testament, too, stops in the middle of things, and history has subsequently continued for two thousand years without God's purpose reaching its fulfillment.

3. THE OLD TESTAMENT STORY IS OUR STORY

The incompleteness of the Old Testament can be seen as a negative—it constitutes its failure. It can also be seen as a positive. The whole Bible story is one that moves from creation through the outworking of human sin to God's achievement of salvation. It is like a play with several acts. The climactic act is the coming of Jesus. The earlier acts are the events described in the Old Testament. But they are all scenes from the same play. Describing the Bible story as a play does not imply it did not happen. Rather, it is just that it has a beginning, a middle, and an end, like a play. All the scenes belong to the same drama. Christians see the earlier scenes as just as much part of their story as the climax is. Although Jesus does not appear till the climax of the story, even the earlier events were overseen by the God and Father of our Lord Jesus Christ who is also Yahweh, the God of Israel.

The New Testament assumes that over the whole Bible one overarching purpose was operative. The Old Testament leads to the New and hints at what becomes explicit there. Often, as in a play, the significance of earlier scenes or remarks can only be fully understood in the light of the denouement in the last act.

Sometimes the Old Testament explicitly looks forward. Many passages in the Prophets see that Israel's present experience, and in particular the way the kings function, does not match up to what God had promised, and these passages look forward to a time when Israel will be put right materially and spiritually, when a real David will sit on the throne. Although the prophecies do look forward, nevertheless they generally see things in terms of a fulfillment or restoration of what the people have lost or never quite experienced. The Prophets do not have a chronological telescope that takes them to Galilee and Jerusalem in Jesus' day. But they affirm the great climax to which the story is to come.

In light of this aspect of the relationship between the Old Testament and the New, Christians read the Old Testament as the earlier part of our story. It also speaks to us as we too live in the midst of a story that is not yet completed. Although the most important event, the coming of Jesus, is passed, we still look forward (as the Old Testament did) to the complete fulfillment of God's purpose for the world.

4. THE OLD TESTAMENT ILLUSTRATES GOD AT WORK

The New Testament assumes that in the Old the same God is at work as in the New, relating to the same people as are spoken of in the New. The church is not a new entity but the rebirth of Israel. So the way God related to Israel in Old Testament times will illustrate how he may be expected to relate to reborn Israel.

While the sacrificial system helps us understand what Jesus was to achieve, the sacrifices were significant in their own right in expressing the relationship between God and his people. The sacrifices burned whole suggest the giving over to God of ourselves and what is precious to us. The fellowship offerings illustrate the relationship of gratitude for prayers answered or just for God's love and provision. The sin offerings remind us of the seriousness of what comes between us and God.

Part of the usefulness of the Old Testament here is that it covers a much wider range of situations than the New. The external circumstances and attitudes of God's people vary over the range of the Old Testament, and sometimes we have more chance of finding ourselves in the Old Testament than in the narrower confines of the New. For instance, the varied descriptions of the rebellions of God's people, especially in Numbers, suggest features that still characterize the life of the church (see 1 Cor 10). Job and Ecclesiastes illustrate believers wrestling with doubt. The Psalms embody the praise and prayer of the people of God, and give us hymns and prayers we can use as well as providing models for the prayer and praise that we compose. Paul declares that "everything written in the Scriptures" (the Old Testament) "was written to teach us, in order that we might have hope through the patience and encouragement that the Scriptures give us" (Rom 15:4).

5. THE OLD TESTAMENT HAS A BROADER RANGE OF CONCERNS THAN THE NEW

The point just made can be extended in another direction. The number of subjects on which the Old Testament has something to say is larger than is the case with the New. The point is illustrated by simply noting where the Old Testament begins, with creation. It explicitly concerns itself with a story set on the widest canvas.

The New Testament refers to creation but does not overtly develop an understanding of the creation relationship between God and the world. It does not need to, because it can presuppose the one in the Old Testament. The strength of the New Testament is that it concentrates all its attention on Jesus. But this is a limitation insofar as it does not tell us so much about God's relationship to the world as a whole.

Because it emphasizes God's creative work, the Old Testament has a positive attitude to the world itself. Although it sees the world as affected by human sin, it still sees it as God's world. It believes that God is the Lord of world history, and it discusses how God is involved in the affairs of the nations—not just insofar as they relate to Israel but for the sake of the nations themselves and of God's own concern for righteousness.

God's involvement with and concern for this world appears also in the Old Testament's burden for righteousness in society, emphasized by the Prophets. The Old Testament does not assume that God is interested only in the soul, the body being merely the dispensable packaging for the really important inner person. It knows that body and spirit were both given by God, that both are to be paid attention to, and that both in the end will be saved. It is concerned with the spirit, with people's relationship with God. It also concerned with bodily welfare and bodily behavior.

The Old Testament's concern with the outward does not mark it as inferior and unspiritual. If God really is the Creator, we can learn from the Old Testament how to have a right concern for and enjoyment of the world.

6. The Old Testament Shows God Condescending to Human Weakness

Although Jesus in Matthew (Mt 5:17) declares that no part of the Torah is to be done away with, he also declares that whereas people were told one thing in the past, he is now telling them something different. Whereas some of the things he refers to that people were told in the past do not come from the Old Testament (for instance, the addition of "hate your enemies" to "love your friends" [Mt 5:43]), most of the commands he discusses here do come from there. The Torah includes provision for divorce; Jesus speaks of divorce as leading to legalized adultery (Mt 5:31-32). The Torah speaks of "an eye for an eye and a tooth for a tooth"; Jesus urges offering the left cheek to the person who slaps the right cheek (Mt 5:38-39).

In both these passages Jesus is asserting a more radical demand than the one the rules in the Torah made. They took a realistic view of the fact that divorces happen and sought to provide regulations to protect the wife. Jesus does not abrogate the law in the sense of saying that there is no need to bother with the wife's protection. He goes deeper into the question and declares that divorce should not happen. Similarly, they took a realistic view of the fact that people seek redress for wrongs done to them and sought to limit that redress (poetically speaking, one black eye, not two, in return for one inflicted). Jesus does not abrogate the Torah in the sense of freeing people like Lamech (Gen 4:23-24) to be as vengeful as they like. He goes deeper into the question and declares that redress is not to be indulged in at all; indeed self-giving is the rule. Nor does he imply that punishment fitting the crime is inappropriate for the law of the land.

The rules in the Torah start where people are. They are given to cope with the kind of eventualities that arise in human society. Jesus comes and says that human society ought to have an entirely different basis. He can say this because his own aim is to give it a new basis. His dying to bring people God's forgiveness and his rising to give them God's Holy Spirit opens up new possibilities for the realization of God's ideal, and this is what he calls us to.

But where is God's ideal revealed? It is revealed in Jesus but also in the Torah itself and elsewhere in the Old Testament. This point is most clearly made in his later discussion of marriage and divorce (Mt 19:1-12). His declaration that in an ideal world divorces will not happen is based not on his own ideas but on the account of the origin of the marriage relationship in Genesis. The Torah itself contains both God's ideal and his condescension to human weakness. Indeed, so does the New Testament, which accepts slavery in a less questioning way than the Old Testament does.

We need both of the ideal and the condescension. We need God's ideal to summon us to the ultimate standard we are called to aim at in Jesus. We need God's realistic lower standard for some insight on how to modify God's ideals to the world in which we have to live. We need them for ourselves too, for although God's forgiveness and God's Holy Spirit are given to us, we carry on living in this age with the pressures of the old nature, and even we might find God's ideals self-defeating if they were all we had. God meets us in our weakness too, and the Old Testament illustrates this.

What is true of the Old Testament is true of the Bible as a whole. It is God's story: it invites us to treat this as our story. It is God's word: it invites us to hear this word as addressed to us.

It is the response of God's people: it invites us to make that response our own.

If you want to work through individual books of the Bible, you could look at the series of paperbacks called "The Old Testament for Everyone" by me and "The New Testament for Everyone" by N. T. Wright.

SCRIPTURE INDEX

Finding the Textbook You Need

The IVP Academic Textbook Selector
is an online tool for instantly finding the IVP books
suitable for over 250 courses across 24 disciplines.

ivpacademic.com